SEPARATE NO MORE

SEPARATE
NO MORE

The Long Road to
Brown v. Board of Education

Lawrence Goldstone

SCHOLASTIC
FOCUS
NEW YORK

Library of Congress Cataloging-in-Publication Data
Names: Goldstone, Lawrence, 1947- author.
Title: Separate no more : the long road to Brown v. Board of Education / Lawrence Goldstone.
Other titles: Long road to Brown v. Board of Education
Description: First edition. | New York : Scholastic Focus, 2021. | Includes bibliographical references and index. | Audience: Ages 12 and up. | Audience: Grades 10–12. | Summary: "Since 1896, in the landmark outcome of Plessy v. Ferguson, the doctrine of 'separate but equal' had been considered acceptable under the United States Constitution. African American and white populations were thus segregated, attending different schools, living in different neighborhoods, and even drinking from different water fountains—so long as the separated facilities were deemed of comparable quality. However, as African Americans found themselves lacking opportunity, barred from the educational, legal, and personal resources readily available to white people, and living under the constant menace of lawless mob violence, it was becoming increasingly apparent that segregation was not only unjust, but dangerous. Fighting to turn the tide against racial oppression, revolutionaries rose up all over America, from Booker T. Washington to W. E. B. Du Bois. They formed coalitions of some of the greatest legal minds and activists, who carefully strategized how to combat the racist judicial system, picking and choosing which cases to take on and how to tackle them. These activists would not always win, in some instances suffering great setbacks, but, ever resilient, they continued to push forward. These efforts would be rewarded in the groundbreaking cases of 1952–1954 known collectively as Brown v. Board of Education of Topeka, in which the U. S. Supreme Court would decide, once and for all, the legality of segregation—and on which side of history the United States would stand. In this thrilling examination of the path to Brown v. Board of Education, Constitutional law scholar Lawrence Goldstone highlights the key trials and players in the fight for integration. Written with a deft hand, this story of social justice will remind readers, young and old, of the momentousness of the segregation hearings"—Provided by publisher.
Identifiers: LCCN 2020009905 (print) | LCCN 2020009906 (ebook) | ISBN 9781338592832 (hardcover) | ISBN 9781338592856 (ebk)
Subjects: LCSH: Brown, Oliver, 1918–1961—Trials, litigation, etc.—Juvenile literature. | Topeka (Kan.). Board of Education—Trials, litigation, etc.—Juvenile literature. | Segregation in education—Law and legislation—United States—Juvenile literature. | African Americans—Civil rights—History—20th century—Juvenile literature. | Civil rights movements—United States—History—20th century—Juvenile literature. | United States—Race relations—Juvenile literature.
Classification: LCC KF228.B76 G65 2021 (print) | LCC KF228.B76 (ebook) | DDC 323.1196/073—dc23
LC record available at https://lccn.loc.gov/2020009905
LC ebook record available at https://lccn.loc.gov/2020009906

1 2020

Printed in the U.S.A. 23
First edition, January 2021
Book design by Abby Dening

To Nancy and Lee

CONTENTS

PROLOGUE

The End of a Long Wait

T HE ENTIRE NATION, even the world, had been fixated for months, but no one could be certain when it would happen.

Every Monday in the spring of 1954, in Washington, DC, spectators had jammed into the gallery of the United States Supreme Court to await the decision of the nine justices as to whether the separation of black children from white children in America's public schools would remain mandated by law. Since 1896, in the landmark case *Plessy v. Ferguson*, the doctrine of "separate but equal"—strict racial segregation—had been ruled acceptable under the United States Constitution. But in five cases that had first been heard in December 1952 and then argued again before nine white men in December 1953, a group of lawyers led by an African American, Thurgood Marshall, had attacked that principle, claiming that no arrangement by which Americans were legally separated by race could possibly be consistent with our most sacred founding document. The decision in those lawsuits, grouped together and known by the lead case *Oliver Brown et al. v. Board of Education of Topeka, Shawnee County, Kansas,* or more simply *Brown v. Board of Education,* would either cement a system that was the centerpiece of white rule in the South—and parts of the North—or be the first step in breaking down that structure and proclaiming racial equality under the law.

So far, the men and women who had sat breathlessly each week, hoping to witness history, had gone home disappointed. No one but the justices themselves and select court personnel knew which cases would be chosen for any given "decision day." (Rulings now are usually issued on Tuesday or Wednesday.) Even after a session began, the roster of cases for that day was not announced, but rather decisions were issued one by one, in whatever order the justices had chosen. *Brown* had yet to be among them.

Expectation had begun to turn to frustration. Even the reporters who had regularly been a part of the crowds had taken to spending their Mondays in the pressroom, one flight down from the courtroom, content to get their information from printed copies of the opinions rather than hearing them read out in person.

May 17 promised to be no exception. Before the session began, reporters were told "it looked like a quiet day." And so, few members of the press were present when the clerk ordered everyone to stand as the justices marched in, led by recently appointed Chief Justice Earl Warren, and then called the court to order with the traditional oration: "The Honorable, the Chief Justice and the Associate Justices of the Supreme Court of the United States. Oyez! Oyez! Oyez! All persons having business before the Honorable, the Supreme Court of the United States, are admonished to draw near and give their attention, for the Court is now sitting. God save the United States and this Honorable Court!"

After the spectators sat, the justices began the day's work. The first case was read, then a second, and then a third. While every case is important, none of these would have anywhere near the national impact of *Brown*. But then, in the pressroom, the Court's information officer, Banning E. Whittington, suddenly put on his coat and told the reporters, "Reading of the segregation decision is about to begin in the courtroom. You will get the opinions up there."

Every reporter bolted out of the room and ran up the stairs.

Brown v. Board of Education is perhaps the most widely recognized Supreme Court case in American history. But for all its renown, most Americans know little about the case itself or the great changes in American society that propelled the Supreme Court to rule as it did.

When *Brown* was argued, *Plessy v. Ferguson* was more

than a half century old, and the crushing Jim Crow laws that the decision had enabled and affirmed had doomed black people throughout the South to a social, political, and economic environment that was simply slavery in a new form. African Americans were denied even the most fundamental rights of citizenship; were regularly jailed, brutalized, and murdered; and could not effectively access a legal system that bragged hollowly about guaranteeing equal rights to all. To make certain that black Americans would remain apart from and inferior to whites, their children were forced into a two-tiered and wholly unequal system of education.

But after America emerged from the Second World War, change began to press itself on American society. For the first time, many whites began to question why their black fellow citizens were treated as people to be shunned, debased, and denied the same opportunities to succeed as they so freely enjoyed. From the military barracks to the baseball field to the courtroom, African Americans had begun to demonstrate that not only could they match the achievements of whites, but they could often exceed them. Still, as of May 17, 1954, segregation remained the law of the land. On that day, the Supreme Court of the United States would decide if it wished to join the march to equality or attempt to stand in its way. No matter what decision they made, the course of American history would be forever changed.

CHAPTER 1

Separate

O N JUNE 7, 1892, Homer Plessy, a thirty-four-year-old shoemaker, purchased a first-class ticket on the East Louisiana Railroad for a thirty-mile journey from New Orleans to Covington, Louisiana. Although the light-skinned Plessy appeared to be nothing more than a well-spoken, well-dressed workingman, he was in fact an *octoroon*, meaning he was one-eighth black. According to an 1890 Louisiana statute, Act 111, known as the Separate Car Law, no one with black blood could ride in railroad cars reserved for whites. Although the law stated that the separate facilities for the two races must be "equal," they never were. People of color were required to ride in the smoky, dingy, broken-down car just behind the locomotive, which became known as the Jim Crow car.

Homer Plessy had not wandered into the whites-only car by accident, nor was he unaware that he was forbidden to be there. He had entered intentionally and had been asked to do so by a group called the Citizens' Committee to Test the Constitutionality of the Separate Car Law. The group had been founded on September 1, 1891, and consisted of doctors, lawyers, newspaper publishers, and prominent businessmen. Almost all were mixed race. Their leader, Louis Martinet, held degrees from both medical school and law school, and edited a local weekly. They had raised $30,000, a large sum of money in those days, to attempt to have the Separate Car Law overturned by the United States Supreme Court.

Louis Martinet and his fellows were part of the most vibrant and accomplished African American community in the South, and perhaps in the entire nation. Since the early eighteenth century, New Orleans, then under French rule, had boasted a population of educated, able, free black men and sometimes women. They referred to themselves as "Black Creoles," or *gens de couleur libres* ("free people of color"). These men and women had prospered both before the Civil War and during Reconstruction; they had sent their children to college; they had visited Europe; some had even owned slaves of their own. The number of free black people in Louisiana—17,462 in 1850—was far greater than in any other Southern state. Fewer than 2,000 lived in neighboring Mississippi.

Although considered "colored" by whites, members of

the New Orleans African American community had often married whites, and after generations, the races had intermingled. Someone half black was called a *mulatto*; quarter black, a *quadroon*; and one-eighth black, like Homer Plessy, an *octoroon*. Octoroons usually appeared so Caucasian that they could come and go in white institutions without anyone questioning their lineage.

And so, after he had been shown to his seat, Plessy informed the conductor of his racial background. The conductor, who could be sent to jail for letting a person of color ride in a white car, instructed Plessy to move to the Jim Crow car. Plessy refused. He was arrested and taken to jail. Everyone involved—the conductor, the police deputy, and Plessy himself—had been courteous and respectful. Bail was soon posted and Plessy released.

The Separate Car Law was only a small part of the assault on African American civil rights by white supremacists in the

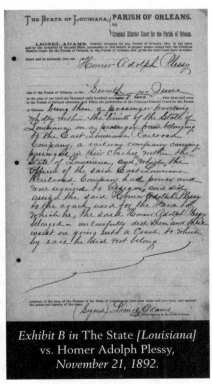

Exhibit B in The State *[Louisiana]* vs. Homer Adolph Plessy, *November 21, 1892.*

South. After the Civil War, states that had been a part of the Confederacy had been forced to draft constitutions giving their black citizens equal rights, but in 1890, beginning with Mississippi, they would draft new constitutions taking those rights away and guaranteeing white rule. With political rights, such as the right to vote, increasingly under threat, the only chance black Americans had of preventing whites in the South from separating them totally from white society—and it was only a small chance—was to persuade the Supreme Court that these new state constitutions and the laws that sprang from them violated their rights as citizens.

So the question became, did forcing African Americans to use separate railroad cars, or separate doors to enter buildings, or to drink from separate water fountains, or to relieve themselves in separate public toilets—or to go to separate schools—violate their basic rights? Or, if the separate facilities were said to be "equal," was forced separation acceptable?

Even before Homer Plessy entered the first-class coach, the Supreme Court had begun to answer that question, and the results were not promising. In 1877, in a case involving separate accommodations on a riverboat, Justice Samuel Clifford had written, "Substantial equality of right is the law of the state and of the United States; but equality does not mean identity . . . there was and is not any law of Congress which forbids such a carrier from providing separate apartments

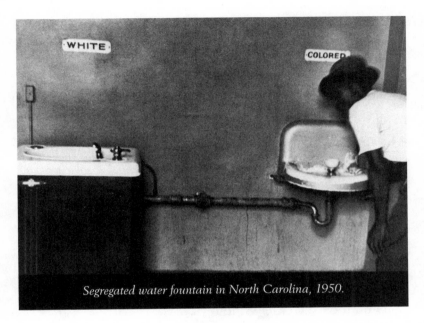

Segregated water fountain in North Carolina, 1950.

for his passengers." And, ominously, although the case had nothing to do with schools, Clifford had added, "Equality of rights does not involve the necessity of educating white and colored persons in the same school any more than it does that of educating children of both sexes in the same school, or that different grades of scholars must be kept in the same school, and that any classification which preserves substantially equal school advantages is not prohibited by either the state or federal Constitution."

Realizing they faced long odds, Martinet and his fellow committee members hired an unusual man to press their case—a white, one-eyed, three-times-wounded Union army veteran and former carpetbagger. His name was

Albion Tourgée, and he had moved from New York to North Carolina in 1865 and become a judge with a reputation for demanding fair treatment for African Americans in his courtroom. When the local Ku Klux Klan threatened his life, Tourgée at first ignored them, but when they menaced his wife and daughter, Tourgée moved back north. He wrote a novel detailing his experiences, *A Fool's Errand by One of the Fools*, which sold over two hundred thousand copies, made Tourgée a good deal of money, and gained him a national reputation. Tourgée saw a Supreme Court test of the Separate Car Law as precisely the sort of cause he wanted to be a part of, and so he accepted Martinet's invitation and took the case without pay.

Since Homer Plessy had been arrested for violating a state law, he had to first go on trial in state court. The judge in the case was John H. Ferguson. At Tourgée's insistence, Plessy's local lawyer, James Walker, did not say that while the facilities were "separate," they were hardly "equal." Instead, he asked that the case be dismissed because the Separate Car Law violated the United States Constitution's Thirteenth Amendment, which forbade slavery, and Fourteenth Amendment, which guaranteed "equal protection of the laws." Judge Ferguson, as expected, refused, and so *Plessy v. Ferguson* was appealed to the United States Supreme Court in April 1896.

In his plea, Tourgée did discuss the obvious inequality

of the facilities available to each race. "The [Separate Car Law] itself is a skillful attempt to confuse and conceal its real purpose. It assumes impartiality. It fulminates apparently against white and black alike. Its real object is to keep Negroes out of one car for the gratification of whites—not to keep whites out of another car for the comfort and satisfaction of the colored passenger." He noted that the law mandated "substantial equality of accommodation," which was obviously lacking on the railroad cars. But then he undercut his own argument, adding that equality of accommodation was not relevant to his constitutional challenge. "The gist of our case," Tourgée insisted, "is the unconstitutionality of the assortment"—meaning the various clauses of the Separate Car Law—"not the question of equal accommodation." In other words, Tourgée was not interested in finding a way around the law but only in having the law struck down entirely.

It was a terrible blunder. Tourgée had denied himself the only strategy that had some small chance of success. The railroads were not pleased with the Separate Car Law because it cost them money to add cars to every train, and so they would not have minded seeing the law overturned. Many of the nine sitting justices on the Supreme Court had worked for railroad companies when they were lawyers. If Tourgée had stressed inequality, the Court might have gone along and agreed that "equal meant equal." Tourgée might then have suggested that if the accommodations were truly equal, they could be swapped. If the Court had approved, since whites would never be willing to spend their journey breathing in smoke and soot in the Jim Crow car, the law would have withered away, with the railroads saving money.

But Tourgée wanted a full constitutional victory or nothing. He would get nothing. To the despair of the Black Creoles, who saw a heritage of learning and achievement more than a century old wiped out, on May 18, 1896, the Court ruled 7–1 that Louisiana's Separate Car Law, and therefore the forced separation of the races, was consistent with the Constitution. Chief Justice Melville Fuller had assigned Associate Justice Henry Billings Brown to write the majority opinion. It was a fitting choice.

Brown was born in South Lee, Massachusetts, a state noted for its opposition to slavery and commitment to equal rights. He wrote, "I was of a New England Puritan family in which there had been no admixture of alien blood for two hundred and fifty years. Though Puritans, my ancestors were neither bigoted nor intolerant—upon the contrary some were unusually liberal."

His father owned lumber mills and, when Henry was eleven, informed his son that he was to become a lawyer. At age sixteen, Henry enrolled at Yale. The college was dingy and grim, with only seven hundred students.

The rooms, though not particularly uncomfortable, were shabby and received but slight attention from the "Professor of Dust and Ashes." All the accessible parts of the woodwork had been profusely illustrated by the pocket knives of former generations. The sanitary arrangements, if such they can be called, were primitive to the last degree. The hours of work were equally so. In winter we rose before dawn, attended morning prayers and a recitation by gaslight, then just introduced into the public rooms, but not into the dormitories, and sat down to breakfast about sunrise. A daily walk to the post office was all the exercise we could afford except on Wednesday and Saturday afternoons. Attendance at chapel twice a day on Sunday was compulsory.

After he graduated in 1856, his father paid for a year's tour of Europe. When he returned, he studied law at Yale and Harvard, leaving, as most law students did at the time, before gaining a degree. He migrated west to seek his fortune in Michigan. Brown secured employment in a local law firm, where he impressed the partners with his diligence and quick mind.

Brown was a grim, stern man given to fits of depression. His eyes were sufficiently bad, perhaps from glaucoma, that for long periods, he could not read and could barely see to get about on the streets. He would lose the sight in one eye in his thirties, and he feared losing sight in the other for the remainder of his life. He avoided military service in the Civil War by hiring a substitute, a common enough practice, but one of which, despite the difficulties with his vision, Brown was apparently ashamed.

During the war, he had remained in Detroit, where business boomed. In 1864, Brown married the daughter of a wealthy lumberman. After the war, he was appointed to the district attorney's office, then to the district court bench, then to appeals court, and finally, in 1890, after fifteen years as a federal judge, he was nominated to the United States Supreme Court. By then, Henry Brown had become known as a fierce defender of property rights.

In his social attitudes, Henry Billings Brown was a man of his time. His views of women, Jews, Native Americans, and Asians were no more generous than his opinion of African Americans. With

Henry Billings Brown.

his opinion in *Plessy v. Ferguson,* Henry Billings Brown, who might otherwise have passed quietly into history, became known for all time as a notorious champion of segregation and racial intolerance.

Brown saw little of merit in any of the plaintiff's arguments. The Thirteenth Amendment claim, that the Separate Car Law imposed "bonds of servitude" on non-whites, he found particularly silly. "The Thirteenth Amendment . . . abolished . . . slavery. Slavery implies involuntary servitude—a state of bondage . . . or at least the control of the labor and services of one man for the benefit of another, and the absence of a legal right to the disposal of his own person, property and services . . . A statute which implies merely a legal distinction between the white and colored races—a distinction which is founded in the color of the two races and which must always exist so long as white men are distinguished from the other race by color—has no tendency to destroy the legal equality of the two races."

Furthermore, Brown insisted, "equality" did not require forcing the races together. He wrote, "In the nature of things, [the Fourteenth Amendment] could not have been intended to abolish distinctions based upon color, or to enforce social, as distinguished from political, equality, or a commingling of the two races upon terms unsatisfactory to either. Laws permitting, and even requiring, their separation in places where they are liable to be brought into contact do not necessarily imply the inferiority of either race to the other." Could not, Brown asked, the needy be served by different institutions than the wealthy? The young different than the old? Boys different than girls? And so, "Gauged by this standard, we cannot say that a law which authorizes or even requires the separation of the two races in public conveyances is unreasonable."

And to demonstrate why that was so, Brown added to the opinion his view of race relations, which was both naive and common, and one which some continue to hold more than a century later. "The argument also assumes that social prejudices may be overcome by legislation, and that equal rights cannot be secured to the negro except by an enforced commingling of the two races. We cannot accept this proposition. If the two races are to meet upon terms of social equality, it must be the result of natural affinities, a mutual appreciation of each other's merits, and a voluntary consent of individuals. If one race be inferior to the other socially, the Constitution of the United States cannot put them upon the same plane."

Only one of the justices, John Marshall Harlan, felt differently. Harlan, a former slaveholder from Kentucky, had long been the Court's greatest champion of equal rights. He used his opinion to produce one of this nation's great declarations of individual liberty and racial equality, but also to destroy the flimsy camouflage laid on by Louisiana and accepted by the majority, that a law mandating separation of the races was not discriminatory since it applied equally to both races:

> It is said in argument that the statute of Louisiana does not discriminate against either race, but prescribes a rule applicable alike to white and colored citizens. But this argument does not meet the difficulty. Everyone knows that the statute in question had its origin in the purpose not so much to exclude white persons from railroad cars occupied by blacks as to exclude colored people from coaches occupied by or assigned to white persons. The thing to accomplish was, under the guise of giving equal accommodation for whites and blacks, to compel the latter to keep to themselves while traveling in railroad passenger coaches. No one would be so wanting in candor to assert the contrary.

Then Harlan declared famously, "In view of the Constitution, in the eye of the law, there is in this country no superior, dominant, ruling class of citizens. There is no caste here. Our Constitution is color-blind, and neither knows nor tolerates classes among citizens. In respect of civil rights, all citizens are equal before the law. The humblest is the peer of the most powerful. The law regards man as man, and takes no account of his surroundings or of his color when his civil rights as guaranteed by the supreme law of the land are involved."

But Harlan's was a lone voice on a court, and in a nation, where few objected to having people of color shunted off so that whites only need

Justice John Marshall Harlan.

interact with them when they needed a waiter, a bellman, a maid, or a janitor. It was a sad but undeniable fact that, for most of white America, North as well as South, separate but equal was not only accepted but welcomed.

CHAPTER 2

Land of Lincoln

WITH VOTING RIGHTS denied and public conveyances secure, Southern state governments proceeded to enact legislation designed to segregate almost every aspect of public life. Georgia passed a public park law in 1905 and within a few years, blacks were excluded from virtually all park facilities throughout the South. Forced segregation was soon mandated at factory entrances, pay windows, movie theaters, restaurants, grocery stores, taverns, and, especially, schools, cemeteries, and public toilets. By 1910, blacks had been effectively herded out of the white South into decrepit, slum-ridden ghettos called "darktowns." To claim that the Jim Crow restrictions were as severe as those for slaves—and much more so than for pre–Civil War free blacks—would in no way be an exaggeration.

With separation came oppression, often violent oppression.

Between 1890 and 1903, 1,889 lynchings were conducted in the United States. In 1,405 of those cases, the victims were black. Although no specific statistics exist, estimates of the number of those lynchings that occurred in Southern states range from 70 percent to 80 percent.

In her pamphlet *Lynch Law in Georgia*, famed anti-lynching crusader Ida B. Wells-Barnett wrote, "During six weeks of the months of March and April just past [1899] twelve colored men were lynched in Georgia . . . The real purpose of these savage demonstrations is to teach the Negro that he has no rights that the law will enforce." Although at first, the violence was largely confined to the South, when African Americans began to move north in search of a better life, violence followed them there.

A particularly ugly incident took place in August 1908 in Springfield, Illinois, a city whose most eminent resident had been Abraham Lincoln. Springfield, in the midst of preparing for a centennial celebration of Lincoln's birth set for the following February 12, was a place of questionable character. "The capital had a reputation, partly justified, of being one of the most corrupt mid-western cities. Vice was a business protected by the authorities and overlooked by the respectable citizens." Springfield was home to fifty thousand residents, 10 percent of whom were black. Although not strictly segregated, most of the black population was clumped in the same neighborhood.

Ida B. Wells-Barnett.

The cycle of events began when a seventeen-year-old black vagrant named Joe James was accused of murdering a white man, Clergy Ballard, after attempting to rape Ballard's sixteen-year-old daughter, Blanche. The incident was reported nationally and newspapers, as they did at the time, played up the incident for maximum shock value. Ballard was described as "cut to pieces by a wild negro while he was defending his home from a fiendish brute who had been caught in his daughter's room," in a crime that "was one of the most cold blooded ever committed in this city."

Details were fuzzy, however. In one account, Blanche Ballard "was awakened by the presence of someone in her room," and evidently she called out. The noise "awakened the father, who sprang from the bed and started for the front door. As he stepped out he met the negro coming around the corner. The negro had a small knife in his hand and with this stabbed Ballard, who was unarmed, thirteen times. The wounded man was hurried to a hospital, where he died at 11 o'clock this morning. The entire north end of Springfield was soon in pursuit of the assassin. James was found asleep by the roadside, his clothes covered with blood and by his side the little knife with which he had committed the deed. The mob fell upon him and would have lynched him but for the prompt arrival of the police."

Another version had Ballard coming upon James outside the house and being sliced repeatedly with a razor in a struggle with the young black man, who admitted to being drunk. James then wandered off, covered with Ballard's blood.

James, who had been released from county jail just two days before the attack, was returned there to await trial. He claimed never to have been in the Ballard house and that his injuries had been caused by the men who set on him when they found him sleeping by the roadside. Black men were regularly accused of crimes of which they were innocent, so whether or not James had actually committed the acts he was accused of will never be known. Still, although "in its attitude toward race relations, Springfield was more Southern than Northern," James did not seem to arouse any further anger from Springfield's white population, and the threat of lynching receded.

This was a relief to local authorities, since dragging black men accused but not convicted of crimes from jail and then murdering them was so commonplace as to be reported casually in the press. On August 6, for example, in Russellville, Kentucky, only three hundred miles from Springfield, the local newspaper reported, "Lodge Members Strung Up," an incident in which "four negroes were taken from jail" by fifty men, and "daylight revealed four bodies hanging from a tree." None of the four had committed a crime, but had been arrested simply for what they were rumored to have said. "The negroes who were lynched were members of a lodge and at a meeting recently it is said they approved the murder of James Cunningham, a white farmer, by a Negro tenant, Rufus Browder."

But then, just as Springfield was settling into its normal routine, another white woman accused a black man of attacking her. Nellie Hallam, wife of a streetcar conductor who worked nights, was "dragged from her bed to an outhouse" by an "unknown negro" and "criminally assaulted." Even worse, "The crime was committed right in the heart of a residence section of the city." But the remedy was at hand. "Several posses are out hunting for the negro and if he is captured there is likely to be a lynching bee."

Mrs. Hallam said she could identify her assailant. Five black men were arrested, but none proved to be the culprit. The next morning, however, George Richardson arrived to mow a nearby lawn, and Nellie Hallam immediately identified him as the man who had broken into her home. Local newspapers seized on the arrest, describing Richardson as a drunken former convict who had served time for murder, when actually he had never been arrested and by all accounts was sober and hardworking. Both Richardson and his wife swore he had been home at the time of the assault, but he was charged with rape and placed in the same jail as Joe James. The local newspapers insisted that something needed to be done about the section of town where African

Americans lived, because it was filled with "scores of worth-less and lawless Negroes."

The presence of two accused black men in the Springfield jail aroused the local whites and they made it clear that neither would live to stand trial. Soon, as many as four thousand of them congregated in the streets in front of the jail. Before he could come under assault, the sheriff, Charles Werner, decided to remove his prisoners, and in that way also remove the reason the mob had gathered at his jail. To create a distraction, he had the local fire brigade ride furi-ously down the street. At the same time, he sneaked the two black men out the back door, where an automobile was waiting. Both men were driven off and safely locked up in state prison.

Instead of quelling the mob's anger, however, being deprived of the chance to murder the two prisoners only inflamed it. Many of the men had been drinking, and at about eight thirty, as it was beginning to get dark, they decided to take revenge. They started by destroying the automobile of the black restaurant owner who was rumored to have driven the prisoners from the jail. Soon the restaurant itself was being bombarded with bricks and bottles. There were shouts of "Curse the day that Lincoln freed the nigger," "Niggers must depart from Springfield," and "Lincoln brought them to Springfield and we will drive them out." The restaurant was soon destroyed, with local police standing about and doing little but smiling at the rioters.

As night fell, although the state militia had been called out, the riot spread. A woman named Kate Howard, "a plump, middle-aged widow whom the local press described as 'a new Joan Arc,'" became one of the ringleaders, spurring the men in the crowd to further violence. When the mayor appeared and pleaded for calm, he was forced to hide in a nearby cigar store, where he remained until the rioting ended hours later.

Men and women of color were attacked throughout the city and their property either burned or destroyed. "Organized groups methodically decimated dozens of black businesses and tenant rooms with bricks, torches, and bullets. Several black residents, either working downtown or who were out at the wrong place at the wrong time, were attacked and beaten." By 1:00 a.m., much of the colored section of the city was in flames. Shots rang out as the rioters discharged their weapons at anyone with dark skin, many with guns stolen from vandalized pawnshops. "Any Negro unlucky enough to be caught by the mob was beaten, including many of the Negro hotel workers in the city, stranded at their jobs when the rioting started. The star pitcher for Springfield's league-leading baseball team was shot in the leg."

Robbed of the opportunity to lynch James and Richardson, the mob seized two other African Americans, one a barber and the other an eighty-four-year-old cobbler, and hanged them both, mutilating the bodies after they were dead. Finally, at three in the morning, sufficient state militia arrived to end the carnage. In the morning, Springfield "resembled a city in wartime." Large sections of the "Badlands," the African American section of town, lay in ruins, at least six black men were dead, as were four white men who had been hit by stray bullets. Dozens had been wounded or injured, and most of the businesses owned by people of color were destroyed. Many homes in which black people lived were burned to the ground as well, while white homes, marked with white handkerchiefs, were spared. Only a large military presence prevented further rioting. "By breakfast time, about 1,800 militia were camped at the arsenal, the capital grounds, and Lincoln Park. The total by Sunday stood at 3,691 men commanded by Major General Edward C. Young."

But the end of the rioting did not close out the affair. Whites were determined to rid Springfield of its black population, many of whom no longer had either homes or employment. "Many firms discharged their Negro help, and others received anonymous threats to do so or else suffer the consequences." More than one thousand African Americans had fled, never to return, most on foot, like a string of refugees after a great battle. Many of those who tried to remain were driven out by threats to the lives of them and their families. Some of the surrounding towns would not allow black families to enter. In one town, Buffalo, a sign was posted at the railway station: ALL NIGGERS ARE WARNED OUT OF TOWN BY MONDAY, 12 M. SHARP. BUFFALO SHARP SHOOTERS. And so some black families were forced to travel in any way they could as far as Chicago or St. Louis to reach safety. In the end, less than half of Springfield's black residents remained in the city.

More than one hundred of the rioters were eventually indicted by a grand jury, but almost all of them on minor charges, such as malicious mischief. Only three were charged with serious crimes, and one of those, Kate Howard, the "new Joan of Arc," killed herself with poison as she was being taken off to jail. Despite overwhelming evidence, only one man was convicted—of burglary, arson, and rioting— but only because he had been foolish enough to confess.

As to the black men, Joe James, protesting his innocence to the end, was tried, convicted, and hanged. George Richardson also insisted he was innocent, but white authorities ignored him. But then, only weeks later, for reasons she never expressed, Nellie Hallam admitted to making up the entire story, most likely to cover up that she had been unfaithful to her husband with a white man. Richardson was freed, lived out his life as a janitor for Bell Telephone, and died peacefully.

The Springfield riot was not the first occasion in which

rampaging whites burned, looted, and murdered, nor would it be the last. But it was unique in one way—it set in motion a chain of events that would culminate on May 17, 1954, in one of the most important Supreme Court decisions in American history.

CHAPTER 3

Resistance

A FRICAN AMERICANS IN the South did not meekly accept their fate and retire willingly into segregation and subjugation. The problem was not the will to resist— there was more than enough of that—but that the game was rigged against people of color. Congress, the presidency, and the courts were controlled by men who believed African Americans to be racially inferior and therefore should never be put on an equal political or social footing with whites. For example, in 1902, when black people were fast being denied the vote and eliminated from the political life of the nation, future president Woodrow Wilson defended the theft of equal rights. "The white men of the South were aroused by the mere instinct of self-preservation to rid themselves, by fair means or foul, of the intolerable burden of governments sustained by the votes of ignorant negroes." Henry Billings

Brown, author of the *Plessy* opinion, wrote in 1906, "No suffrage, no nigger."

With those in power lined up against them, and few effective tools of resistance available, African Americans were forced to try to grasp shreds of power wherever they could. While many in the black community stepped forward to try, two men in particular became the leaders of this seemingly hopeless effort. One of them would try to use the Springfield riot to help propel the movement forward with increased momentum, and the other, the most famous black man in America, would resist.

On September 18, 1895, the Cotton States and International Exposition in Atlanta, Georgia, celebrated its opening day. This gala trade fair was meant to attract business both from the North and across the Atlantic to what organizers called the "New South." It was billed as the region's largest and most important event since the end of the Civil War, a display of progress and prosperity, featuring six thousand exhibits, costing $2 million to produce, and expected to attract as many as one million visitors during its three-month run.

Peace and reconciliation between North and South were prominent themes. In his welcoming speech, Judge Emory Speer proclaimed, "This is indeed a happy day for the country. Cold and dull must be the nature of that man who is insensible to these convincing proofs gathered that the world may see the advancement of our people on all the paths trending toward a more perfect civilization." He noted that Civil War veterans from both sides mixed freely, reminiscing and sharing tales of war and the subsequent peace.

Another theme was portraying the New South as a place of racial harmony. Speer exclaimed, "I here declare the so-called 'race question' does not exist. There are millions of colored people who live and who will live among many more millions of white people. Why shall anyone forge a race issue?" To further convince skeptics that the South harbored no ill feelings toward black people, the fair sponsored a "Negro Building" designed and built by people of color, and designated December 26, five days before the fair closed, as "Negro Day."

As final proof of their goodwill, the organizers invited a black man to speak during the opening ceremonies. For this honor, they chose a forty-year-old educator named Booker T. Washington, described as the "principal of the Tuskegee Alabama Normal and Industrial School," which was devoted to training young black men and women in teaching and the mechanical arts. Little was known about Washington at the time, but Americans soon learned that he had been born a slave and, through education and hard work, had risen to lead a respected institution and become what white people liked to term "a credit to his race."

Booker T. Washington.

❖

The reaction in the Northern press to this unique invitation was everything Southern whites could have hoped for. "The selection of Booker T. Washington . . . to make an address at the opening of the Atlanta Exposition, is an almost unparalleled tribute to Mr. Washington personally, and to the negro race of which he is such a distinguished representative. Had any one predicted twenty-five years ago that the South would so honor a negro, he would have been looked upon as a madman."

Washington took full advantage of the opportunity. Striking just the right balance between conciliatory and proud, Washington expressed acceptance of whites' assertions that black Americans, only thirty years removed from slavery, were not yet ready for full equality, or even in most cases the right to vote. (He would, however, fiercely defend the principle that both races be subject to the same conditions for voting rights.) He also accepted segregation as a path to prosperity for both races. "In all things that are purely social we can be as separate as the fingers, yet one as the hand, in all things essential to mutual progress."

He counseled black Americans to stop thinking in grandiose terms but rather focus on building themselves up from the bottom to share in "a new era of industrial progress." "The wisest among my race understand that the agitation of questions of social equality is the extremest folly, and

Washington and guests at the Tuskegee Institute in Alabama.

that progress in the enjoyment of all the privileges that will come to us must be the result of severe and constant struggle rather than of artificial forcing . . . It is important and right that all privileges of the law be ours, but it is vastly more important that we be prepared for the exercise of these privileges. The opportunity to earn a dollar in a factory just now is worth infinitely more than the opportunity to spend a dollar in an opera-house . . . Our greatest danger is that in the great leap from slavery to freedom we may overlook the fact that the masses of us are to live by the productions of our hands, and fail to keep in mind that we shall prosper in proportion as we learn to dignify and glorify common labor, and put brains and skill into the common occupations of life."

Although this part of his speech is often overlooked, Washington was also trying to convince white employers to hire men and women of color, rather than white immigrants from Europe. Speer, in his welcoming speech, had made a point of noting that the New South was the perfect place for hardworking Europeans to settle, a workforce that could close off one of the few areas of opportunity for black workers.

The reaction to Washington's speech was resoundingly positive. The *New York Tribune*, for example, wrote,

Washington speaking in 1915.

"When [men] think of American freedom, they can do no better than to think of Booker T. Washington's oration at Atlanta." Within months, Washington's embrace of the American ideal of hard work had made him a national celebrity, at least in white society. White leaders agreed that slow, steady progress, coupled with education and honest toil, was the best way for people of color to ease their way into the mainstream of American life, although they continued to favor hiring fellow whites when they could.

Washington would become a favorite of wealthy industrialists such as John D. Rockefeller and Andrew Carnegie—Carnegie would give Washington $150,000 as a personal gift. In 1901, Washington would publish an autobiography, *Up From Slavery*, to almost universal acclaim and booming sales; he would lecture to white audiences across the nation; he would help found the National Negro Business League, to promote entrepreneurship and financial independence; he would have tea with Great Britain's Queen Victoria; and he would even be invited to the White House for dinner with President Theodore Roosevelt.

As his acceptance by whites increased, however, Washington began to arouse the ire of some men and women of color, who believed members of their race were being bought off with scraps, and who took issue with Washington's unwillingness to challenge a rising tide of white oppression. One of them was a brilliant scholar and activist named William Edward Burghardt Du Bois, who had initially praised Washington's speech but later wrote, "His efforts at appeasement had led the whites to the very aggressions he was trying to check."

W. E. Burghardt Du Bois (pronounced Doo Boyz) was born in 1868 in Great Barrington, Massachusetts, only a few miles west of Henry Billings Brown's boyhood home in South Lee. He was his high school's valedictorian at sixteen and graduated from Fisk University in Nashville, Tennessee, at twenty, spending his summers teaching in African American schools in the area. He got an additional bachelor's degree in history from Harvard in 1890, where he was a commencement speaker, and then a master's degree the following year. For two years after that, Du Bois was given a scholarship to study history and economics in Germany, at the University of Berlin. He returned to Massachusetts and, in 1895, the same year as Booker T. Washington's Atlanta Exposition speech, became the first African American to be granted a Harvard doctorate. His doctoral dissertation, "The Suppression of the African Slave Trade to the United States of America, 1638–1870," was published by the university.

Du Bois taught history and sociology at Wilberforce University in Ohio and spent a year as a researcher at the University of Pennsylvania, before accepting a professorship in economics and history at Atlanta University in

W. E. B. Du Bois as a young man.

1897, where he would remain on the faculty until 1910. In a remarkable output of essays, articles, histories, and even novels, Du Bois attacked segregation, racism, lynching, and the widespread belief among whites that African Americans were racially inferior. In 1903, he published a groundbreaking work of history and sociology, *Souls of Black Folk*, a series of essays and sketches, that explored a variety of themes, including the role of black people in American life, how they were viewed by white people, and how they viewed themselves. There had never been anything written by an African American, not even Frederick Douglass, that combined the passion, the ferocious attack on racism, the breadth of scholarship, the insight, and the academic excellence of Du Bois's work.

In one of the chapters, "Of Mr. Booker T. Washington and Others," Du Bois calls Washington's approach the "Atlanta Compromise" and accuses him of "practically accepting the alleged inferiority of the Negro races." He added, "There is among educated and thoughtful colored men in all parts of the land a feeling of deep regret, sorrow, and apprehension at the wide currency and ascendancy which some of Mr. Washington's theories have gained."

His attack on Washington and his policies was both fierce and unprecedented. "His doctrine has tended to make the whites, North and South, shift the burden of the Negro problem to the Negro's shoulders and stand aside as critical

and rather pessimistic spectators; when in fact the burden belongs to the nation, and the hands of none of us are clean if we bend not our energies to righting these great wrongs . . . But so far as Mr. Washington apologizes for injustice, North or South, does not rightly value the privilege and duty of voting, opposes the higher training and ambition of our brighter minds—so far as he, the South, or the Nation, does this—we must unceasingly and firmly oppose them."

Du Bois also accused Washington of wanting to be the only voice of the black community, of insisting that his strategy be the only strategy, and so the two men became enemies. From there, Du Bois would continue to attack Washington, and Washington would do all he could to undermine Du Bois. That conflict became acute in 1905, when Du Bois decided to found an organization of African American intellectuals, members of what was called the "Talented Tenth," to work for equal rights far more aggressively than Booker T. Washington's slow-steady approach. The first meeting, which was to be held in secret, would be in Fort Erie, Ontario, a few miles south of Niagara Falls, and so their work became known as the Niagara Movement.

Dozens of invitations were sent out, and as the nation's foremost black intellectual, Du Bois had every reason to believe just about all of them would be accepted. But through his contacts, Washington learned of both the meeting and

The Niagara Movement founders. Top row: H. A. Thompson, New York; Alonzo F. Herndon, Georgia; John Hope, Georgia; unidentified. Second row: Fred McGhee, Minnesota; unidentified boy; J. Max Barber, Illinois; W. E. B. Du Bois, Atlanta; Robert Bonner, Massachusetts. Bottom row: Henry L. Baily, Washington, DC; Clement G. Morgan, Massachusetts; W. H. H. Hart, Washington, DC; and B. S. Smith, Kansas.

who had been invited. Since he enjoyed almost total support of whites in the North, where most of the funding
for black colleges and social programs came from, he or
his white friends exerted pressure on the invitees to ignore
Du Bois's call. Only twenty-eight showed up at Fort Erie. But
Du Bois was convinced those twenty-eight would be the
base of a new, more radical movement for equal rights and
justice. "The Niagara Movement was the first national organization of Negroes which aggressively and unconditionally
demanded the same civil rights for their people which other
Americans enjoyed."

Their program could not have stood in greater contrast
to the Tuskegee approach. Du Bois's platform was a series
of demands, not requests. They included freedom of speech
and criticism, including of the Washingtonians; a free press,
able to arouse black America and free them from being a
captive race; universal male suffrage, with guaranteed political participation on the same basis as whites; the end of all
social and political distinctions based simply on race, which
were termed "unreasoning human savagery"; a high school
or trade school education for anyone who wanted it and
government subsidies for black colleges; equal employment
opportunities and an end to race discrimination by labor
unions; and leadership in the black community by those who
would bring these goals to fruition.

Not only was this approach against everything Booker

T. Washington stood for, he feared white philanthropists might cease to actively support his efforts and switch their allegiance to the Niagara Movement. So Du Bois had to be stopped. "Since the day of its inception, Booker Washington scrutinized the movement and plotted its destruction." He used all his influence in the press and among white and black activists to belittle and discredit Du Bois, everything from accusing him of inflating the number of attendees to demanding newspaper and magazine editors condemn the new group. He even attempted to use spies to keep him abreast of what Du Bois was doing. As a result, by the end of 1905, the Niagara Movement had grown to only 150 members.

The following year, the conference was held in Harpers Ferry, West Virginia, site of abolitionist John Brown's failed attempt to incite a slave rebellion, for which Brown was later hanged by the United States government. This meeting attracted a larger group, and even some women, including Ida B. Wells-Barnett. In addition to *Lynch Law in Georgia*, she was the author of similar tracts as *Southern Horrors: Lynch Law in All Its Phases* and *The Red Record: Tabulated Statistics and Alleged Causes of Lynching in the United States*. Wells-Barnett was a tireless and impassioned advocate for legislation and government action to prevent a horrific practice that, while illegal, was almost never punished in the North, and never at all in the South. But, although she shared Du Bois's opinion of Booker T. Washington, she was also fiercely independent, and her willingness to work within an organizational structure was always in question.

Du Bois attempted to set even a greater distance between himself and Washington. "We claim for ourselves," he declared, "every single right that belongs to a freeborn American, political, civil, and social; and until we get these rights we will never cease to protest and assail the ears of America." But this second conference was also a disappointment. Du Bois and his associates once again did all they could, but short of funds, with no real ability to bring any of their program to fruition, and a powerful enemy determined to stop them, the Niagara Movement failed to gain traction.

Although Washington and Du Bois shared a personal dislike, and Washington was openly trying to destroy the Niagara Movement, it would be a mistake to see Washington as acting just for selfish, personal motives. He genuinely believed that his strategy of gradual economic growth was the only path to equality for his people and that the radicals threatened racial progress. And Washington had a long record of opposing discriminatory laws in the South, where different standards were applied in the law to blacks and whites. Still, it is equally clear that he had grown rigid, unwilling to accept even the possibility that Du Bois or those like him had valid points to make.

And so, as summer 1908 began, it had become clear to everyone, except possibly W. E. B. Du Bois, that the Niagara Movement would soon fail entirely.

But then, thousands of whites burned and murdered blacks in Springfield, Illinois, and everything changed.

CHAPTER 4

From the Ashes in Springfield

THE SPRINGFIELD RIOT was front-page news across America. The *New York Times*, for example, on August 15, began with the headline "Illinois Mobs Kill and Burn. Foiled in Attempt to Lynch Two Negroes, Angry Whites Start Destructive Raid. Mob Sets Fire to Negro District and Refuses to Allow Fire Department to Work. Two Known Dead, Many Hurt." The next day's headline read, "Rioters Hang Another Negro. Mobs, Defying 3,000 Soldiers, String Up Old and Innocent Victim. Threaten All Blacks. Governor Declares Martial Law, but Situation Grows Worse on Second Day." And then, finally, on August 17, "Troops Check Riots. Sixth Victim Dies."

These headlines achieved what Du Bois and the Niagara Movement had not—they convinced a number of wealthy, influential white men and women that a new, more robust effort was needed in the push for equal rights. Booker T.

Washington's program was not abandoned, but many in the white community began to understand that even if his strategy were eventually successful, many innocent people of color would die and be brutalized while they waited for genuine progress.

One of these was a wealthy, thirty-one-year-old Harvard Law School graduate from Louisville, Kentucky, named William English Walling. "English," as he was known to his friends, was a descendant of slave owners and the grandson of the Democratic candidate for vice president in 1880. After law school, he became a socialist, moved to New York, and became involved in progressive causes, such as workers' rights and racial equality. Walling traveled with his wife to Springfield after the riots and wrote a newspaper article, "The Race War in the North," in which he vividly described the bloody assault while thousands of Springfield's white citizens, "including many women and children, and even prosperous business men in automobiles calmly looked on."

William English Walling.

He concluded that "the spirit of abolition must be revived," or Southern bigots will have succeeded in "transferring the race war to the North." The article ended, "Yet who realizes the seriousness of the situation, and what large and powerful body of citizens is ready to come to their aid?"

One of the people who read Walling's article was a suffragette and social reformer, Mary White Ovington. "For four years I had been studying the status of the Negro in New York. I had investigated his housing conditions, his health, his opportunities for work. I had spent many months in the South, and at the time of Mr. Walling's article, I was living in a New York Negro tenement on a Negro Street. And my investigations and my surroundings led me to believe with the writer of the article that 'the spirit of the abolitionists must be revived.'"

Ovington contacted like-minded friends who met informally in New York City. "It was then that the National Association for the Advancement of Colored People was born. It was born in a little room of a New York apartment." But the organization was still just an idea. They agreed, however, that the hundredth anniversary of Abraham Lincoln's birth, February 12, 1909, should be the official founding date for whatever they eventually established.

From there, Ovington, along with *New York Evening Post* editor Oswald Garrison Villard, grandson of famed abolitionist William Lloyd Garrison, and a number of others organized a two-day conference beginning on May 31,

1909, to create what they called the "National Negro Committee," an odd name for a group of people almost entirely white. Villard extended an invitation to Booker T. Washington to attend the meetings, although he knew Washington would object to an agenda he would see as too "radical." When Washington

Mary White Ovington.

declined to participate—he was, he said, more interested in "progressive, constructive work" for the race, rather than in "agitation"—Villard contacted the man he really wanted: W. E. B. Du Bois. Du Bois accepted immediately, as did a number of Niagara Movement board members. The conference drew three hundred men and women, mostly white but many of color, who, as the *New York Times* noted, "conferred as equals," and "Negro men and white women sat side by side."

Du Bois, who called the conference "the most significant event of 1909," wrote in his notes, "Mary White Ovington suggested to Walling and Oswald Garrison Villard that a conference be called in New York and that white friends of the Negro be invited and also those who had organized and were supporting the Niagara Movement." After the meeting, Du Bois wrote, "The N. A. A. C. P. was organized out of this conference and the Niagara Movement held no further meetings. There was no formal merger, but seven of the charter members of the Niagara Movement went on the Board of Directors of the new organization and practically all of the membership was represented on the Advisory Committee."

The committee had forty members, most of them white, but including both Du Bois and Ida Wells-Barnett. (Wells-Barnett would leave the organization two years later because she felt it was not sufficiently radical and that an organization devoted to black civil rights should not have white leaders.) Under the banner "National Negro Committee, 500 Fifth Avenue, New York, New York," the Group of Forty issued an official platform—and a solicitation for contributions—which began, "We denounce the ever-growing oppression of our 10,000,000 colored fellow citizens as the greatest menace that threatens the country." To try to persuade Washington and his followers to support them, they added, "We agree fully with the prevailing opinion that the transformation of unskilled colored laborers in industry and agriculture into skilled workers is of vital importance," but also, "we demand for the Negroes, as for all others, a free and complete education," which included "an academic education for the most gifted." Although Washington continued to oppose the new strategy, the tide was moving against him.

The group gathered momentum and at their second annual meeting on May 12, 1910, the committee adopted the formal name of the organization, the National Association for the Advancement of Colored People. Du Bois recommended *colored* instead of *Negro* to signify the association's interest in advancing the rights of all dark-skinned people. The goals of the NAACP were the abolition of segregation, discrimination, disfranchisement, and racial violence, particularly lynching.

Other than Du Bois, who was made director of publicity and research, all the senior officers were white, including Walling, Villard, and John E. Milholland, who had made a fortune in business and had previously been one of Booker T. Washington's major benefactors. (Washington, as it turned out, had been correct in his fears that Du Bois would attract away his white supporters.) For president, the group chose Moorfield Storey, sixty-seven years old, white, and with a record of opposing abuses of power the equal of anyone in America. As a young man, he had served as secretary to abolitionist Senator Charles Sumner, had gone on to a distinguished career in constitutional law, served as president of the American Bar Association—where he forced the ABA to admit black lawyers by threatening to resign if they did not—had opposed American imperialism in the Philippines and Cuba, and had been a champion of women's rights and equal rights for people of color, including Native Americans.

Although there were some who insisted the president of the National Association for the Advancement of *Colored* People actually be of color, Du Bois was not among them. He seized on the opportunity the new position brought him to begin a magazine called *The Crisis: A Record of the Darker Races.* "When W. E. B. Du Bois founded *The Crisis* in 1910, as the house magazine of the fledgling NAACP, he created what is arguably the most widely read and influential periodical about race and social injustice in U.S. history. Written for educated African-American readers, the magazine reached a truly national audience within nine years, when its circulation peaked at about 100,000."

In his first editorial, Du Bois wrote, "The object of this publication is to set forth those facts and arguments which show the danger of race prejudice, particularly as manifested today toward colored people. It takes its name from the fact that the editors believe that this is a critical time in the history of the advancement of men." He would edit *The Crisis* for twenty-five years, making it the most important vehicle for African American writers and artists in American history. It smashed racist stereotypes by publishing accounts of the many achievements of men and women of color in all walks of life, while at the same time detailing harsh tales of discrimination and harrowing accounts of lynchings.

THE CRISIS

RECORD OF THE DARKER RACES

Volume One — NOVEMBER, 1910 — Number One

Edited by W. E. BURGHARDT DU BOIS, with the co-operation of Oswald Garrison Villard, J. Max Barber, Charles Edward Russell, Kelly Miller, W. S. Braithwaite and M. D. Maclean.

CONTENTS

PUBLISHED MONTHLY BY THE

National Association for the Advancement of Colored People

AT TWENTY VESEY STREET — NEW YORK CITY

ONE DOLLAR A YEAR — TEN CENTS A COPY

The cover of the first issue of The Crisis.

Along the Color Line

POLITICAL.

THE "grandfather" clause of the Arkansas Constitution reads as follows:

"SECTION 4a. No person shall be registered as an elector of this State, or be allowed to vote in any election held herein, unless he be able to read and write any section of the Constitution of the State of Oklahoma; but no person who was on January 1, 1866, or at any time prior thereto, entitled to vote under any form of government, or who at that time resided in some foreign nation, and no lineal descendant of such person, shall be denied the right to register and vote because of his inability to so read and write sections of such Constitution.

"Precinct election inspectors having in charge the registration of electors shall enforce the provisions of this section at the time of registration, provided registration be required. Should registration be dispensed with the provisions of this section shall be enforced by the precinct election officers when electors apply for ballots to vote."

This amendment has been voted upon and the votes canvassed, but an official count has not been announced, and probably will not be until just before the general election in November.

The Hon. J. C. Napier will replace the Hon. W. T. Vernon, of Kansas, as Register of the United States Treasury. The Chattanooga *Times* gives the following reasons for the change:

"It appears now that Vernon has outlived his usefulness, since he could not help the administration to stem the insurgent wave that recently swept over the Sunflower State, and that his reappointment was contingent on his success in that campaign. It is learned from that day he was marked for retirement.

"Tennessee Republican politicians readily recognized the opportunity to make a master stroke and impression on the Negro vote in Tennessee, by recognizing one of their race with an important office.

"Napier for eight years was a member of the Republican State Committee, but the white members fell out with him at the recent state convention when it was believed that he had agreed to use his influence with the Negroes in favor of Patterson. Since he was deposed the committee has been without Negro membership, and this sop is held out to pacify the rebellious Negroes all over the state."

Senator Cummins, of Iowa, will introduce a bill into Congress for direct primaries in selecting candidates for President and Vice-President. He says:

"To me the injustice is plain of permitting the 4,000 Republicans of Mississippi to cast 20 votes in the convention, while Iowa, with 300,000 Republicans, can cast only 26. Is it right that Georgia, with only 30,000 Republican voters, should have exactly the same number of delegates as Iowa, with ten times that number of Republican votes? Every one recognizes that the Republican party—such as it is in the far Southern States—is composed almost wholly of Federal officeholders and those who want Federal office. It has been demonstrated time and time again that the delegates to Republican national conventions from these states are absolutely venal and that they uniformly vote with the administration forces, which purchase them by means of postoffices and collectorships."

The United Colored Democracy of the State of New York has been organized for the coming campaign. They demand a colored regiment in the New York National Guard, and also colored policemen and firemen.

J. C. Manning and the progressive Republicans in Alabama are fighting Mr. Washington's political influence in that state.

The newly elected Governor of South Caroline, Blease, made his fight on a platform opposing Negro education and prohibition.

The Negroes of South Carolina gained complete control of the State Republican Convention.

The Hon. P. B. S. Pinchback, once Reconstruction Governor of Louisiana, has been appointed to the Internal Revenue Service in Cincinnati, O.

The Colored Independent Political League has decided to support the Democratic ticket in Ohio, New York and New Jersey; the Republican tickets in Delaware and West Virginia, and to favor Senator Bulkeley, of Connecticut, and oppose Senator Lodge, of Massachusetts. Local Independent organizations are at work in New York, Ohio, New Jersey, Utah and Missouri.

The National Executive Committee of the Socialist party have appointed Lena Morrell Lewis and George A. Goebel a committee of two to investigate the condition of the Negro in America.

Suit has been brought in the United States Circuit Court to compel the city of Annapolis, Md., to register colored voters. Annapolis by city ordinance has attempted to nullify the Fifteenth Amendment.

In the second issue, Du Bois wrote an exposition on prejudice and discrimination that is timeless. "What is the National Association for the Advancement of Colored People? It is a union of those who believe that earnest, active opposition is the only effective way of meeting the forces of evil. They believe that the growth of race prejudice in the United States is evil. It is not always consciously evil. Much of it is born of ignorance and misapprehension, honest mistake and misguided zeal. However caused, it is nonetheless evil, wrong, dangerous, fertile of harm. For this reason it must be combated. It is neither safe nor sane to sit down dumbly before such human error or to seek to combat it with smiles and hushed whispers. Fight the wrong with every human weapon in every civilized way."

Which was exactly what the new group set out to do.

CHAPTER 5

To the Courts

WHATEVER HIS COLOR, the choice of Moorfield Storey to head the NAACP was equally significant because for the first time a national, coordinated effort to attack Jim Crow was to be spearheaded by one of the most prominent lawyers in the United States, and one who intended to use all his skill and all his training to defeat the enemies of equal rights.

Although that crusade would eventually lead directly to the Supreme Court building in May 1954, Storey and his colleagues began much more simply. Soon after the organization was founded, they took up not a great constitutional issue involving thousands, but the murder conviction of one man.

In 1907, South Carolina had "peonage" laws that bound black workers to white employers with labor contracts that were simply slavery by another name. Pink Franklin, an

African American sharecropper, had signed such a contract with Jake Thomas, but he had fulfilled its terms and accepted another contract with a different white farmer. In July 1907, Thomas claimed that Franklin owed him for wages that had been advanced and swore out a warrant for Franklin's arrest with a local magistrate. The magistrate agreed, even though a federal judge, William Brawley, had declared the peonage laws unconstitutional just two months before. He dispatched a local constable, Henry Valentine, who went to the shack where the twenty-two-year-old Franklin lived with his twenty-one-year-old wife, Patsy.

Valentine recruited another man to accompany him to Franklin's shack before dawn, where, without announcing who he was or why he was there, he burst through the door while the Franklins were asleep and opened fire. Franklin and his wife were both wounded. But Franklin, who had been hit in the shoulder, grabbed his pistol and returned fire, striking Valentine in the stomach. The constable collapsed to the ground and would die later that day. The deputy fled and Franklin and Patsy fled as well, just ahead of a lynch mob that had formed as soon as the deputy reached town.

Franklin and his wife were eventually sheltered by white officials who wanted to avoid a lynching, and he was taken to state prison. He and Patsy were tried on September 9, 1907, and despite pleas of self-defense and testimony by the deputy that Valentine had burst into the building without announcing himself, Pink Franklin was convicted by an all-white jury and sentenced to hang. Patsy was found not guilty. Franklin's lawyers, both black, appealed to the state supreme court, insisting that since jurors were chosen according to voting rolls, which included almost no black men, Franklin could not get a fair trial. The appeal was denied. The lawyers then appealed to the United States Supreme Court, which also rejected Franklin's claim.

But the Supreme Court case was not decided until May 1910, by which time the NAACP was looking for equal rights cases they could get involved in. Franklin was scheduled to be hanged on December 23, 1910, and they saw his case as exactly the sort of issue they could use to publicize injustice. Since there was no possibility of overturning the verdict, they focused on getting Franklin's sentence commuted to life imprisonment, from which they could then attempt to secure a pardon. *The Crisis* ran an article on the case in its very first issue and would continue to do so in almost every subsequent issue. Du Bois wrote, "If the law is based on common sense and if a man has the right to protect his home against unlawful attack, then the burden of establishing legal authority for an assault upon a home must rest upon the assailants, and not upon the householder." He added, "Let justice be done."

Led by the NAACP's executive secretary, Frances

Blascoer, and South Carolina lawyer Thomas Miller, a petition with more than one thousand signatures was presented to the court, as were letters recommending commutation that had been obtained from a number of prominent white officials, including President William Howard Taft. Even the judge at Franklin's trial strongly recommended that Franklin not hang. On December 17, only six days before Pink Franklin was to die, the governor granted a stay of execution, and two weeks later, on January 5, 1911, he commuted Franklin's sentence to life imprisonment. The NAACP kept on the case and, although it took eight more years, in 1919, Pink Franklin received his pardon. Once free, he changed his name to Mack Rockingham, moved with Patsy to a new town, had two sons, and lived as a farmer until his death in 1949.

After success in the Franklin case, Moorfield Storey set his sights on a bigger prize, one that would resound across the nation and establish the NAACP as the most important equal rights organization in America.

When Oklahoma was granted statehood in 1907, it drafted a state constitution in which it allowed men of all races to vote, as required by the United States Constitution's Fifteenth Amendment. In 1910, however, the state approved an amendment that stated, "No person shall be registered as an elector of this State or be allowed to vote in any election herein, unless he be able to read and write any section of the constitution of the State of Oklahoma," something which few African Americans and many poor whites could not do. But to make sure that those poor whites did get to vote, the amendment went on to say, "but no person who was, on January 1, 1866, or at any time prior thereto, entitled to vote under any form of government, or who at that time resided in some foreign nation, and no lineal descendant of such person, shall be denied the right to register and vote because of his inability to so read and write sections of such constitution." This provision was known as a "grandfather clause," because it allowed those who would otherwise have been disqualified—in this case, illiterate whites—to be able to register if their grandfather, or some other direct fore-bear, had voted. This clause would not apply to black people, since before 1866, almost all had been slaves and of course unable to vote.

Oklahoma was not the first state to employ a grandfa-ther clause as part of a program to deny the vote to men of color. (Women were not yet allowed to vote no matter what their color.) Beginning with Mississippi in 1890, every Southern state, by then back under the control of white supremacists, would draft new constitutions, employing a variety of tactics—literacy requirements, poll taxes, resi-dency or employment requirements among them—designed to keep African Americans off the voting rolls. But many of these, a literacy requirement, for example, would also take the vote away from poor whites. To allow them to continue to vote without letting black voters back in, beginning with Louisiana in 1898, five former secessionist states—which included Alabama, Georgia, North Carolina, and Virginia— wrote grandfather clauses into their state constitutions.

But the grandfather clause was considered risky and encountered a good deal of opposition among white supremacists in each of the states in which it was eventually adopted. Many thought it *so* obvious that the Supreme Court, which had upheld all sorts of contrivances, might actually balk at this one. But it was also remarkably effective and convenient to apply, so the risks were thought worth taking.

After its adoption in Oklahoma, almost no black voters were allowed to register for the November 1910 congressional elections, and since almost all African Americans voted Republican, the Democrats—the party of white supremacy in those days—succeeded in adding a congressional seat. James Harris, chairman of the state Republican Party, lodged an official complaint with the United States Department of Justice, also headed by a Republican. A number of state voting officials, all Democrats, were then indicted for enforcing the grandfather clause and violating African Americans' Fifteenth Amendment guarantee not to be denied the right to vote on account of race. When the case came to trial, another Republican, federal judge John H. Cotteral, agreed. The grandfather clause was unconstitutional. If his decision held, grandfather clauses in the other Southern states would be void as well.

After Judge Cotteral's ruling, two of the registrars, Frank Guinn and J. J. Beal, were convicted of conspiracy to deprive men of color of the right to vote and were sentenced to a year in jail each. They appealed the conviction, which went to the Supreme Court in a case that would become known as *Guinn v. United States*. Although African Americans had won some voting rights cases, this was the sort they usually lost. The Court had pretty much allowed states to set voting eligibility as they saw fit. State constitutions in Mississippi, Louisiana, and Alabama, drawn up expressly—and publicly—to make certain almost no black men would be allowed to vote, had been approved by the justices in Washington.

While the case would be presented to the Court by the United States solicitor general—the federal government's lawyer—Moorfield Storey was allowed to file a brief in support of the government position. This was the first time the NAACP had participated in a Supreme Court case, and the stakes were high. The case was heard in October 1913, but almost two years passed before the Court rendered its decision. Finally, in June 1915, a unanimous Court ruled that the grandfather clause was "repugnant to the Fifteenth Amendment and therefore null and void." The opinion was written by Chief Justice Edward D. White, a Louisiana native who had fought for the Confederacy during the Civil War.

Although winning in the Supreme Court was a milestone, the decision had almost no practical effect. Neither Guinn nor Beal served jail sentences, and the Oklahoma legislature met in special session almost immediately to revive the grandfather clause. This they did by passing a law that allowed anyone registered in 1914—in other words, whites who had been grandfathered in—to be automatically registered to vote. African Americans had only a two-week window to register—with the literacy requirement still in place—or they would lose the right to vote forever. Although that law was also eventually overturned by the Supreme Court, it was not until 1939. Other states in which the grandfather clause had been invalidated found new ways to keep black voters off the voting rolls as well.

Still, for the first time since Reconstruction, the Supreme Court had become at least a potential ally in the fight for equal rights, and the NAACP had made it so. It can never be known, of course, how the justices would have ruled had Moorfield Storey not filed his brief, but never had a lawyer of his position and reputation taken such a stand before the Court.

Less than six months after the NAACP's victory in *Guinn v. United States*, Booker T. Washington died. He was only fifty-nine. Whatever his disputes with Du Bois and the

NAACP, he left a legacy of honesty and self-sufficiency that he pursued with honor and zeal virtually up to the day of his death. Du Bois wrote, "The death of Mr. Washington marks an epoch in the history of America. He was the greatest Negro leader since Frederick Douglass, and the most distinguished man, white or black, who has come out of the South since the Civil War."

But his passing left a void that the NAACP leadership quickly moved to fill. The following year, at Du Bois's initiative, the NAACP called a conference at Amenia, New York, inviting a number of Washington's followers in an attempt to unite the equal rights movement. Almost sixty people from both organizations attended, and when they were done, the NAACP was to be the only voice with which the organized equal rights movement spoke.

That same year, the NAACP returned to the Supreme Court, this time not as an interested bystander but as a direct participant, with Moorfield Storey arguing before the justices himself. Equally important was that William Warley, who, like Homer Plessy, was intentionally creating the dispute, was an official of the NAACP.

At issue was a 1914 Louisville, Kentucky, city ordinance that prohibited African Americans from living on blocks in which the majority of residents were white, and whites from living in houses on blocks where the majority was black. Baltimore had passed a similar law in 1910, and about a dozen other Southern cities had followed suit. Louisville claimed it was justified in passing such a law to protect against race conflict and promote "public peace."

The plan was to have a real estate agent, Charles Buchanan—who happened to be an NAACP supporter— sell a building lot on a majority white block, to William Warley, a newspaper editor and president of the newly formed Louisville chapter of the NAACP. The block they chose was near a number of other blocks where black owners were a majority, and so whites had taken to dumping homes on the market when African Americans moved nearby. The agreed price for the lot was $250, but Warley withheld $100 because, he said, the city ordinance would not allow him to occupy the house as a residence, which lowered the value of the property because he could not live in the house himself.

With whites unwilling to buy the lot and African Americans forbidden to, Buchanan's property was worthless. Buchanan, the white real estate agent, sued Warley, the African American buyer, for violating their contract. But in his suit, he also claimed the city ordinance had deprived him of his property without due process of law, in violation of the Fourteenth Amendment. The courts in Kentucky refused to void the ordinance, and so, in 1916, *Buchanan v. Warley* was heard in the United States Supreme Court. This would have seemed a straightforward case, except for two things. The first was that although Moorfield Storey was

The fourth annual conference of the NAACP.

one of the lawyers, he was appearing for Charles Buchanan, the white plaintiff, and arguing against the black defendant, William Warley. The second was that although segregation was the obvious target, neither Storey's nor Warley's lawyer discussed racial discrimination at all. They cast the case entirely on the question of property rights, about which the justices were extremely sensitive. Storey's main argument was the Court should uphold "the common law right of every landowner to occupy his house or to sell or let it to whomever he pleases."

The strategy worked perfectly. In a unanimous decision, the Court held that the black defendant, Warley, did not have the right to withhold full payment from the white plaintiff, Buchanan. But the justices also ruled, as the NAACP had hoped, that the city of Louisville, not technically a part of the case, could not restrict who could sell what to whom. "We think this attempt to prevent the alienation of the property in question to a person of color was not a legitimate exercise of the police power of the State, and is in direct violation of the fundamental law enacted in the Fourteenth Amendment of the Constitution preventing state interference with property rights except by due process of law." And so, Moorfield Storey and the NAACP had created the first constitutional exception to segregation since *Plessy v. Ferguson.*

Once again, the Court's ruling did not end housing

discrimination or even come close to doing so. But one brick had been kicked out of the foundation of "separate but equal," and there seemed a clear path to taking aim at others. It would take many decades and involve a changing cast of brave and dedicated men and women—and sometimes children—but *Buchanan v. Warley* would eventually lead right to the doors of America's schoolhouses.

CHAPTER 6

The Red Summer

THE CRUX OF Jim Crow politics was to wall off people of color from white society, making certain they could not assert their rights as citizens and keeping them subservient to their white masters. Incredibly, most whites, both North and South, also expected black people to be patriotic Americans, grateful for the blessings of freedom and democracy. For a time, it even seemed to work, but eventually that very patriotism on which whites insisted eroded the subservience on which they relied.

The process began in Europe. With the coming of the First World War in 1914, and America's entry in the conflict in 1917, two areas of opportunity suddenly opened for African Americans. The first was the military. The United States Army was undermanned and so a call went out for recruits, even black recruits. The army was strictly segregated and black soldiers were subject to enormous abuse, but still many thousands answered the call. Most were assigned to menial tasks in the United States, but some were sent to Europe to fight. Before the war, most whites thought African Americans lacked both the discipline and the bravery to be effective soldiers, but black men in combat shattered that myth. One unit, the 1st Separate Battalion, was assigned to the French Army and fought with such distinction that they were awarded the Croix de Guerre, one of France's highest military honors.

Even more gratifying to black soldiers was that in France, where almost all of them were stationed, they were not treated as if they were members of a subhuman race but rather as equals, almost celebrities. To the fury of white American soldiers and officers, *les soldats noirs* were often pursued by French women, which led to the Americans spreading false rumors of widespread rape, the same sort of accusation that worked so well in the United States. But the French, both men and women, found the gossip ridiculous, which incited white Americans even more.

The second opportunity for African Americans was in industry. As the nation moved to a war footing, demand for goods to supply the soldiers increased. But the war also drastically reduced the number of immigrants from Europe, who had been the main source of labor in Northern factories. With an increase in the demand for labor and a decrease in supply—at least white supply—Northern industrialists were willing to employ men and women of color. Black families forced to toil in the white man's fields in the South sensed opportunity and began to move north in what would later be called the Great Migration. The Pennsylvania Railroad signed up ten thousand black workers from Georgia and Florida alone, and more than seventy-five thousand were hired to work in coal mines. Northern cities, where many of the factory jobs were located, began to creak under the strain of so many immigrants seeking housing, food, and city services. Since Northern whites were no more eager to live near black people than those in the South, urban ghettos began to form. But even underpaid and abused, many black people earned more in a year working in Northern industries than they had in ten years working in the Jim Crow South. And with higher earnings came increased dignity.

When the war ended on November 11, 1918, returning soldiers mixed with black industrial workers to create a combustible brew, and in the summer of 1919, it exploded.

Black men who had served in the military and been treated with respect by foreigners returned home to the same abuse and deprivation as before they left but, in many cases, were far less willing to tolerate it. In May 1919, Du Bois wrote in *The Crisis*, "By the God of Heaven, we are cowards and jackasses if now that that war is over, we do not marshal every ounce of our brain and brawn to fight a sterner, longer, more unbending battle against the forces of hell in our own land. We return. We return from fighting. We return fighting. Make way for Democracy! We saved it in France, and by the Great Jehovah, we will save it in the United States of America, or know the reason why."

The black industrial workers who had for the first time been compensated for at least some of what their work was worth were often the first to be fired when war demand evaporated. That left them unemployed or underemployed in urban ghettos, which quickly succumbed to poverty and crime, leaving whites with a reinforced vision of black inferiority, never for a moment thinking they were blaming the victim. But many whites lost their jobs as well and soon the competition for vastly reduced resources turned to violence.

Almost three dozen cities, among them Chicago, New York, Philadelphia, Baltimore, Omaha, and Washington, DC, experienced riots in late spring, summer, and early fall of 1919, some of them horrific. Dozens were killed, hundreds wounded, and vast numbers of homes and businesses destroyed. James Weldon Johnson, a field officer for the NAACP and soon to be its executive secretary, toured some of the scenes of bloodshed and called it the Red Summer. The Red Summer events were unlike earlier such incidents when unarmed African Americans were massacred by white supremacists—in many cases in 1919, black men, some back from the war, some from the factory floor, fought back.

In Chicago, the fighting lasted thirty-eight days, and in Washington, DC, for the first time ever, there were more whites killed than blacks. But mostly, it was again African Americans who bore the brunt of the violence.

Nowhere was the carnage worse than in Phillips County, Arkansas. In September, a group of African American army veterans began to organize black tenant farmers into a union to demand a better method of determining how much money they should be paid. The sharecroppers had been regularly cheated for years. They called their group the Progressive Farmers and Household Union of America. On the night of September 30, 1919, at a church in Hoop Spur, approximately one hundred of the sharecroppers were attending a meeting of the group, when a sheriff and a deputy stopped outside and began to shoot wildly through the windows. The black men inside fired back, killing the deputy and slightly wounding the sheriff.

The sheriff swore out a posse of three hundred angry white men, and the governor added three hundred national guardsmen, who then swept through the county for a week, killing and brutalizing every black person they could find. Some of the black men fought back, but it was hopeless. More than two hundred blacks were killed, and five white men died as well, most probably killed accidentally by friendly fire. All the black men who had not been killed or had escaped, more than seven hundred, were rounded up and tossed into a stockade. Those who swore to work for almost nothing and never again make trouble were released, and those who refused were kept in custody. Sixty-seven were eventually sent to prison, and twelve men thought to be the ringleaders were put on trial for first-degree murder. Prisoners were tortured to confess or testify against others. Alf Banks, one of the twelve, told his lawyer, "I was frequently whipped and also put in an electric chair and shocked and strangling drugs would be put in my nose to make me tell that others had killed or shot at white people and to force me to testify against them." The twelve were convicted by an all-white jury, with a mob howling for their blood both in the courthouse and out in the street. All were sentenced to hang. Many others were given life imprisonment. The trials took less than ten minutes each.

The NAACP sent Walter White to see if anything could be done. White, although identifying as African American, had blue eyes, blond hair, and a fair complexion. Posing as a white newspaper reporter—he was given press credentials by the *Chicago Daily News*—White gained an interview with the governor, who called him "one of the most brilliant newspapermen he had ever met," and then headed to Phillips County. White pretended to be sympathetic to the white rioters and so had no trouble getting local people to talk to him. But then he wrote articles that appeared in *The Crisis* and other publications, detailing the massacre

The African American defendants on trial after the Arkansas riot of 1919.

of African Americans and showing that the sentences were simply a court-sponsored lynching.

Contributions poured in from across the nation to mount appeals—they would reach $50,000 before the case was completed—and the NAACP hired lawyers, both white and black, to help plead the case. As always, they lost in state court. When the case reached the United States Supreme Court in 1922, Moorfield Storey, again the lead counsel, claimed that the mob outside the building made a fair trial impossible, and even without the mob, the proceeding was a mockery with just about every right guaranteed to any defendant under the Constitution violated. The Court had never overturned the result in a criminal trial on such grounds, and rarely on any grounds, but this time it did.

On February 19, 1923, in *Moore v. Dempsey*, by a 6–2 margin, Justice Oliver Wendell Holmes wrote, "If the whole case is a mask—that counsel, jury and judge were swept to the fatal end by an irresistible tide of public passion, and the state courts refuse to correct the wrong, then nothing can prevent this court from securing to the petitioners their constitutional rights." The cases were sent back to state court, and all twelve condemned men were eventually freed, as were the sixty-seven who had been sentenced to prison. Mob justice had finally been dealt a blow.

The result was a triumph for Walter White and the

Walter White.

NAACP, but just missed being a tragedy. Even before his articles were published, word got out that the fair-skinned Northern reporter who pretended to be sympathetic to whites was actually colored. One day, as he later told it:

> I walked down West Cherry Street, the main thoroughfare of Elaine, on my way to the jail, where I had an appointment with the sheriff, who was going to permit me to interview some of the Negro prisoners. A tall, heavy-set Negro passed me and, sotto voce [in a low voice], told me as he passed that he had something important to tell me, and that I should turn to the right at the next corner and follow him. Some inner sense bade me obey. When we had got out of sight of other persons, the Negro told me not to go to the jail, that there was great hostility in the town against me and they planned harming me. In the man's manner there was something which made me certain he was telling the truth. Making my way to the railroad station, I was able to board one of the two trains a day out of Elaine. When I explained to the conductor—he looked at me so inquiringly—that I had no ticket because delays in Elaine had given me no time to purchase one, he exclaimed, "Why, Mister, you're leaving just when the fun is going to start! There's a damned yaller nigger

down here passing for white and the boys are going to have some fun with him."

I asked him the nature of the fun.

"Wal, when they get through with him," he explained grimly, "he won't pass for white no more."

CHAPTER
7

Passing the Torch: The New Negro Movement

ALTHOUGH *MOORE V. DEMPSEY* did not end racial violence, as *Buchanan v. Warley* had not ended housing segregation, and *Guinn v. United States* had not restored the right to vote, creating a legal footing for a continued assault on "separate but equal" was a necessary first step. These cases also provided opportunities for a new generation of black leaders to begin to take control of the NAACP.

Walter White was one who saw his star shine. From his articles and activities in Arkansas, he became a nationally known figure. He would eventually be named to head the NAACP and remain in that position until his death in 1955. Another of the movement's rising stars was James Weldon Johnson, who became executive secretary of the NAACP in 1920—White's predecessor—the first African American other than W. E. B. Du Bois to occupy a senior position in the organization. Johnson was a poet and novelist, had been a diplomat in Central and South America, a professor at New York University, an anti-lynching crusader, had taught the children of former slaves in the South, and was the first African American admitted to the Florida bar.

Another product of the NAACP's advances was a surge of interest among African Americans in black culture and pride in the successes of members of their race. *The Crisis*, beginning in its very first issue, had featured a column, "Along the Color Line," which highlighted achievements of African Americans in the arts, academics, law and medicine, business, and items Du Bois called "Social Uplift." One note, for example, in the May 1915 issue, under "Education," read, "Charles H. Houston, a colored senior of Amherst College, has been elected to the Phi Beta Kappa." Houston had also been class valedictorian. He would become a good deal more.

By the 1920s, black culture was becoming more and more visible in white society, no more so than in New York City, called the "Culture Capital" by James Weldon Johnson. New York experienced an explosion of African American art, theater, and music that came to be known as the Harlem Renaissance. Although most of the activity was centered in that most famous of African American urban districts, some of it began to move downtown. African American actors were cast in Broadway plays, jazz became immensely popular, artists such as sculptress Meta Vaux Warrick Fuller and painter Aaron Douglas highlighted the black experience, and writers such as Langston Hughes and Zora Neale Hurston were widely read.

In 1925, African American writer Alain Locke published *The New Negro*, a collection of essays, poems, and short stories that attacked race prejudice and ridiculed common stereotypes applied to African Americans by whites. "For generations in the mind of America," Locke wrote in the opening essay, "the Negro has been more of a formula than a human being—a something to be argued about, condemned, or defended, to be 'kept down,' or 'in his place,' or 'helped up,' to be worried with or worried over, harassed or patronized, a social bogey or a social burden." But all that was changing. "The younger generation is vibrant with a new psychology; the new spirit is awake in the masses, and under the very eyes of professional observers is transforming what has been a perennial problem into the progressive phases of contemporary Negro life . . . we are achieving something like a spiritual emancipation."

Locke's work spread quickly through the black community and spawned what became known as the New Negro Movement. The subservient approach of Booker T. Washington was dead, replaced by a commitment from black Americans to claim what the Constitution promised, not beg for it.

Oddly, for much of the Harlem Renaissance, for which *The New Negro* became almost an anthem, Locke did not

Alain Locke.

live in New York, but rather in Washington, DC, where he chaired the philosophy department at Howard University and also taught classes on race relations.

Howard—named for the Union general who headed the Freedmen's Bureau after the Civil War and was instrumental in creating a school of higher learning for black students— was, and still is, the finest traditionally black college in the nation. Beginning in 1929, one of Alain Locke's fellow faculty members was the man who more than any other was responsible for the legal attacks that made *Brown v. Board of Education* possible.

New Negro literary figures (from left) Langston Hughes, Charles S. Johnson,
E. Franklin Frazier, Rudolph Fisher, and Hubert T. Delany, posing on the roof of
580 St. Nicholas Avenue, Harlem, on the occasion of a party in Hughes's honor in 1924.

❖

Charles Hamilton Houston was born in Washington, DC, on September 3, 1895, the son of a successful lawyer and the grandson of slaves. From boyhood, he was trained by his parents to be a leader, and he did not disappoint.

He attended M Street High School (later renamed Dunbar), which, although it was segregated, was among the finest public high schools in DC. Houston distinguished himself academically and was accepted to Amherst College in Massachusetts, where, as *The Crisis* reported, he graduated with honors at age nineteen, magna cum laude, as a valedictorian and was made Phi Beta Kappa. He returned to Washington, DC, to teach English at Howard University, but with the coming of World War I, he was one of the thousands of African Americans who put country over bigotry and enlisted in the army.

Houston was sent to Iowa, to the army's first black officers' training camp, and was commissioned a second lieutenant. He was soon sent to France, assigned, of course, to a segregated division. In Europe, Houston was one of those who experienced firsthand the radical contrast in their treatment by European whites with that of their white countrymen. "As a Second Lieutenant overseas, he encountered virulent racism practiced by Red Cross workers, white enlisted men, and his fellow white officers. Because of his race and color, he suffered arbitrary insults, indignities and exposure to mortal danger." In one incident, he was attacked by some white soldiers and only barely escaped being lynched. His experience overseas, as it would for many black soldiers in the next war, set him on his life's path. "The hate and scorn showered on us Negro officers by our fellow Americans convinced me that there was no sense in my dying for a world ruled by them. I made up my mind that if I got through this war I would study law and use my time fighting for men who could not strike back."

When he was discharged from the army in 1919, during the Red Summer, Houston applied to Harvard Law School, where he was quickly accepted. There, he became the first black student to edit the *Harvard Law Review*, after which he graduated with a doctor of laws degree in 1923. One of his instructors was future Supreme Court justice Felix Frankfurter. Upon graduation, Houston was granted a scholarship to observe legal practices in Europe and North Africa. When he returned, he joined his father in the renamed law firm of Houston and Houston.

Most of the cases the Houstons took on were day-to-day legal matters, such as deeds, contracts, and property disputes. Although white clients had any number of white lawyers from whom to choose for these services, men and women of color had almost none. Soon afterward, Mordecai Johnson, who had just been appointed president of Howard University, the first African American to hold that title, asked

Charles Houston.

Houston to teach at the law school. At the time, the law school provided only the very basics of legal training—classes were held at night and the faculty was not accredited by the American Bar Association. But Houston accepted. Although he knew that in his law practice he was providing essential legal services to members of a race who could not ordinarily have access to them, he began to feel more and more that he should attack the roots of discrimination, not just its results. The best way to do that, he was convinced, was to create a new generation of highly skilled black lawyers.

"The social justification for the Negro lawyer as such in the United States today is the service he can render the race as an interpreter and proponent of its rights and aspirations," Houston wrote later. "There are enough white lawyers to care for the ordinary legal business of the country if that were all that was involved. But experience has proved that the average white lawyer, especially in the South, cannot be relied upon to wage an uncompromising fight for equal rights for Negroes. He has too many conflicting interests, and usually himself profits as an individual by that very exploitation of the Negro which, as a lawyer, he would be called upon to attack and destroy." And the need was acute. "There are not more than 100 Negro lawyers in the South devoting full time to practice: 100 Negro lawyers to care for the rights and interests of 9,000,000 Southern Negroes or approximately one Negro lawyer to every 90,000 Negroes."

After he began to teach, Houston could see firsthand how inadequately most African American lawyers had been trained, and as a result were ill-equipped to effectively fight for their clients in court. But he would soon have the opportunity to change all that.

Mordecai Johnson had not offered Charles Houston a teaching position by accident. When Johnson accepted the job of president of Howard University in 1926, then no more than a "glorified high school," it was with the intention of shaking things up, of producing a quality stream of black graduates from what many black intellectuals called "Dummies Retreat." Almost immediately, he hired a series of first-rate scholars, such as Ralph Bunche, E. Franklin Frazier, and the great historian John Hope Franklin.

But to create the sort of nationally recognized institution of higher learning he sought, Johnson needed to improve the graduate programs as well, especially the law school. Supreme Court justice Louis Brandeis had told him, "I can tell most of the time when I'm reading a brief by a Negro attorney. You've got to get yourself a real faculty out there or you're always going to have a fifth-rate law school. And it's got to be full-time and a day school."

Which was exactly what Charles Houston had in mind. When Johnson offered him the job of assistant dean in 1929—the same year Moorfield Storey died at age eighty-four—Houston accepted not simply to create a law school that might coexist with the seven white law schools in Washington, DC, but to compete with them—and to win. "Despite criticism, he insisted on 'unqualified excellence' from faculty and students and worked 'with singleness of purpose [and] unremitting drive' for the conversion of the Howard Law School . . . to a full-time, nationally known and respected school of law accredited by the American Bar Association and the Association of American Law Schools." The speed with which he achieved that shocked both the Howard University administrators and white lawyers in Washington. One of the lawyers Houston brought in to teach, William Hastie, who had also gone to Amherst and Harvard Law School and would later be a federal judge, said that in five years, Houston achieved "a transformation which ordinarily requires a generation in the history of an educational institution."

Houston altered the curriculum, making equal rights a priority, and personally taught the first course in civil rights law ever offered at an American law school. Although he had recruited a first-class faculty, to make certain the teaching was up to his exacting standards, Houston took charge of the education of the most promising students himself. One of them was a tall, gangly, exceptionally bright twenty-two-year-old from Baltimore who loved to argue and who did not seem to have much respect for authority.

Thurgood Marshall.

CHAPTER

8

The Challenge

O BTAINING EQUAL RIGHTS in court was going to be a bigger challenge for Charles Houston and his fellow black lawyers in the 1930s. Two Supreme Court decisions did as much or more harm to their cause than their victories had done them good.

The first, one of Moorfield Storey's rare losses, effectively undid one of his biggest victories. In 1922, a white woman named Irene Corrigan signed a contract to sell her house on S Street NW in Washington, DC, to a prominent physician, Arthur Curtis, and his wife, Helen, both African American. But the previous year, most of the block's white homeowners, Corrigan included, had signed an agreement not to sell or rent to an African American or to allow a black person to occupy their property in any way. When another of the white homeowners, John J. Buckley, heard of the sale, he sued Corrigan, claiming she had breached the contract.

Corrigan claimed that the agreement had been made in violation of the United States Constitution and was therefore void. *Buchanan v. Warley*, after all, had made such restrictions illegal if initiated by a state or local government, and the principle of allowing a person to do what they wanted with their own property seemed the same.

But the local courts disagreed and said they had no power to overturn an agreement made by private individuals. Irene Corrigan, with the backing of the NAACP, appealed, and in 1926, after three years, *Corrigan v. Buckley* was heard by the Supreme Court. Although the Court did not rule specifically on the case, the justices, as in the lower courts, unanimously agreed that they had no right to interfere with a private contract. The lower court ruling, then, which allowed race-based discrimination by private individuals, would stand.

The impact went beyond Irene Corrigan not being able to sell to Dr. Curtis. It meant that in order to achieve segregated housing, all whites needed to do was to draw up private agreements to keep their neighborhoods free of people of color, which by the thousands they proceeded to do.

Equally devastating was a Supreme Court decision upholding school segregation against a family that approved of school segregation. In 1924, in Bolivar County, Mississippi, Gong Lum, a local storekeeper of Chinese descent, attempted to register his nine-year-old daughter, Martha, in an all-white elementary school. The school principal told Lum that his daughter had to attend the black school, although Martha was academically advanced and the conditions at the black school were far inferior. Lum decided to sue. He claimed he and his daughter had been denied "equal protection of the laws," as guaranteed in the Fourteenth Amendment, but even more that because Martha was not "black," she should be able to attend a white school. The Mississippi Supreme Court disagreed, ruling that, as a "Mongolian" or "yellow," Martha was "colored," and therefore could be required to attend a "colored" school.

Gong Lum appealed to the United States Supreme Court and, in a unanimous decision in *Gong Lum v. Rice*, the justices ruled that, under *Plessy*, Mississippi could decide who went to what schools and who was white and who was not. Chief Justice (and former president) William Howard Taft wrote, "The case reduces itself to the question whether a state can be said to afford to a child of Chinese ancestry, born in this country and a citizen of the United States, the equal protection of the laws, by giving her the opportunity for a common school education in a school which receives only colored children of the brown, yellow or black races . . . but we think that it is the same question which has been many times decided to be within the constitutional power of the state Legislature to settle, without intervention of the federal courts . . . The decision is within the discretion of the state in regulating its public schools, and does not conflict with the Fourteenth Amendment."

Gong Lum was a crushing defeat. It meant not only that the Supreme Court had endorsed racial segregation in public schools, but that Southern states could run those schools almost entirely as they wished, including deciding who went where and how much money would be devoted to black schools versus white.

And money spent on black schools was next to nothing. By the 1930s, Alabama was spending $37 to educate a white child, but only $7 per student for African Americans. The figures in Georgia were $32 versus $7; in Mississippi, $31 and $6; and in South Carolina, $53 and $5. Teacher salaries, availability, and quality of textbooks and the school buildings themselves all reflected the funding differences.

The American Council on Education conducted a survey of African American schools in the Jim Crow South in the late 1930s. The report of the investigators was shocking.

"The homes of rural Negro youth are, with few exceptions, dismally inadequate. Their schools, which have the support of the state, are scarcely better. Unattractive schools and a lack of supplies for class work do little to inspire pupils with aesthetic feelings or to induce teachers to put forth their best efforts. Teachers on a bare subsistence income, and often with a minimum of preparation, are hardly qualified to foster the development of wholesome, well-adjusted personalities in their pupils."

Comparisons of schools black children in the South

An African American schoolhouse near Summerville, South Carolina, 1938.

were forced to attend with Charles Houston's M Street High School were heartbreaking.

A typical rural Negro school is at Dine Hollow, Alabama. It is in a dilapidated building, once whitewashed, standing in a rocky field unfit for cultivation. Dust-covered weeds spread a carpet all around, except for an uneven, bare area on one side that looks like a ball field. Behind the school is a small building with a broken, sagging door. As we approach, a nervous, middle-aged woman comes to the door of the school. She greets us in a discouraged voice marked by a speech impediment. Escorted inside, we observe that the broken benches are crowded to three times their normal capacity. Only a few battered books are in sight, and we look in vain for maps or charts. We learn that four grades are assembled here. The weary teacher agrees to permit us to remain while she proceeds with the instruction. She goes to the blackboard and writes an assignment for the first two grades to do while she conducts spelling and word drills for the third and fourth grades. This is the assignment:

"Write your name ten times.

Draw an dog, an cat, an rat, an boot."

That any child could emerge from such a system with enough of an education to do anything but toil in the fields or work in the most menial of jobs was a near impossibility. But that, after all, was the point. Without education, Southern African Americans would never be able to challenge a social order that kept them in such grueling, low-paying work, where they could help make white people rich generation after generation, in a prison of ignorance from which there was no escape.

It was to create this avenue of escape, to make it possible for black children to achieve more than their parents and to live better lives—and to be in the position to help other African Americans to do the same—that the NAACP set as its goal.

CHAPTER 9

To the Courts Once More

CHARLES HOUSTON TOLD his most famous student, "Doctors can bury their mistakes but lawyers can't." Thurgood Marshall added, "And he'd drive home to us that we would be competing not only with white lawyers, but really well-trained white lawyers, so there just wasn't any point in our crying about being Negroes."

But Houston also knew that his students would need to compete not only with other lawyers but with judges who saw African Americans as inferior and a body of law, especially Supreme Court law, that encouraged whites to treat black people that way. This made the problem of ending legal segregation in schools that much more difficult. There did not seem to be any real avenue open from which to attack. Segregation itself had been affirmed in *Plessy*, and a series of later decisions, including *Gong Lum*, seemed to allow states to pass any laws they chose to enforce a system that could not have been more obvious in its intent to discriminate. How would it be possible, then, to end a system of discrimination that had the approval of the highest court in the land to do the very thing it was being asked to outlaw?

Both Houston, working from the Howard University Law School, and the NAACP saw two possible glimmers of hope. First, black Americans, at least to a degree, had entered mainstream white society in a growing number of pursuits, particularly in the arts, and had shown themselves to be nothing like the stereotypes white racists had been putting forth for decades. This was also true in the law, where black lawyers had become a much more common presence, even in the South, and, although often lacking in training, had proved themselves smart and capable advocates for their clients.

The second was more practical. In 1922, Charles Garland, a Harvard student from a prominent white family, used his $800,000 inheritance to establish the American Fund for Public Service and soon afterward left Boston to become a farmer. Eventually, $100,000 from what was usually called the Garland Fund was donated to the NAACP to be used to mount a legal campaign against racial discrimination, especially in schools. At the recommendation of both Felix Frankfurter, by then a Supreme Court justice, and Charles Houston, the NAACP hired Nathan Margold, white, Jewish, and, like Houston, a former student of Frankfurter at Harvard Law School, to become the group's official attorney and to draw up a plan.

Margold eventually produced a three-part, 218-page report, but the section he delivered in May 1931 was the most important. Although every Supreme Court segregation decision had upheld the practice, Margold proposed attacking the problem differently. His analysis of Jim Crow schools in every state in the South confirmed that while they were certainly separate, they were hardly equal. The only way separate schools could be made equal was either to take money away from white schools and spend it on black schools, or for Southern school districts to increase the money they spent on education to bring black schools to parity. The first would be out of the question to the white racists who ran Southern state and local governments. The second was unequally unlikely. In 1931, the United States was in the middle of the Great Depression, when the American economy collapsed, millions were unemployed, and many thousands lost their homes or their farms, and no Southern school district was going to bankrupt itself in support of black education.

So Margold's strategy was not to attack segregation as a system—as tempting and just as that may have been—because the money to see such a legal challenge through was simply not there. (The Depression had struck at the NAACP as well. When the stock market crashed, almost all the money from the Garland Fund was lost, leaving only $10,000 with which to take on Jim Crow.) Instead, Margold proposed targeting segregation as practiced, one school district at a time, to "boldly challenge the constitutional validity of segregation if and when accompanied irremediably by discrimination." He would select school districts where the educational facilities were so unequal as to make it obvious that the school boards had violated the law, and there were hundreds of those districts to choose from.

But the point was not to win small, stand-alone victories against individual school boards, to "fritter away our limited funds" to change policy in a handful of districts, but to build up a body of law that could later be used to invalidate segregation as a practice. Margold would make the point over and over that segregation could not exist without inequality—that "separate" and "equal" could not exist together—and so the *Plessy* doctrine must fall. In addition, Margold believed that the more cases African Americans won to overturn school inequality, the more they would become mobilized to test other aspects of Jim Crow rule, and the more whites would be forced to treat them with respect.

The Margold Report became the centerpiece of the NAACP strategy, its "bible," according to William Hastie. Said Thurgood Marshall many years later, "His report stayed with me. It's still with me." But when Nathan Margold left the NAACP in 1933 to take a job in the United States

Department of the Interior, Walter White, by then the head of the organization, needed to find the right man to implement his strategy. He turned to Charles Houston. It took White two years of persuading, but in 1935, Houston agreed to leave Howard, move to New York, where the NAACP headquarters was located, and become its lead lawyer.

Houston agreed with Margold's overall strategy but thought Margold had been too optimistic about winning cases against Southern school boards. There were simply too many defenses, however flimsy, against treatment that seemed unequal but that whites could insist was not. They could claim there were not enough pupils to justify more spending on black schools, or that because even very young

The NAACP headquarters in New York City, circa 1936.

black children had to work, the pupils of school age would not attend anyway. Each of these was either false or a direct result of Jim Crow discrimination, but proving it in a courtroom could take more time and money than the NAACP could afford.

Although Houston recognized that the most important place to end school segregation was at the beginning, in elementary school, he chose the other end of the educational spectrum as his starting point. He decided to narrow the focus to areas of education about which there could be no debate about separate being unequal—graduate and professional schools. Since there were almost no medical or law schools for black students in the South, the NAACP would make the case that states would have to choose between providing equal graduate schools for its black students—which would be extremely expensive—or to allow African Americans into existing white-only schools. The ultimate goal would be for the United States Supreme Court to rule on enough of these cases to bring school segregation down of its own weight.

The first challenge would be on behalf of Donald Murray, a would-be law student, to be argued in Maryland, where Charles Houston's most famous student, Thurgood Marshall, had been denied entry to the law school because of his race. Representing Donald Murray with Charles Houston before the Maryland Supreme Court would be that same Thurgood Marshall.

CHAPTER 10

Thurgood Marshall Joins the Fray

THOROUGHGOOD MARSHALL, NAMED for his grandfather, was born on July 2, 1908, in Baltimore, Maryland. His father, Will, a waiter, first on the railroad, then at a country club, served white men and women, and his mother, Norma, an elementary school teacher, educated black children. Like most African Americans in Maryland, Thoroughgood, who in second grade shortened his name to Thurgood, was descended from slaves, although both his grandfathers had served as free men in the United States military.

His parents never had much money, but they lived in a well-kept and relatively prosperous neighborhood in West Baltimore. Neither had been to college—Will had never even graduated from high school, although Norma returned to school after her sons were born—but each was extremely curious and intellectually vibrant, and they instilled in

Thurgood and his older brother, Aubrey, a deep respect for learning. On his days off, Will Marshall sometimes took his sons to the local courthouse, to sit with them in the colored section and observe the process of ordered argument that led to a decision, sometimes on the merits of the case but often because of the skill of one of the lawyers. At home, the family discussed the United States Constitution over the dinner table.

The lessons took. Although Thurgood was social and a bit mischievous—and loved to argue—he was also serious and thoughtful. The wife of his local pastor recalled, "I can still see him coming down Division Street wearing knee pants, with both hands dug way into his pockets and, kicking a stone in front of him, to visit his grandparents at their big grocery store. He was in deep study, that boy, and it was plain something was going on inside him."

Aubrey, who was quieter and less argumentative, would go on to medical school and become a surgeon, but Thurgood seemed made for the law. "Marshall later said his father, who demanded he prove every claim he made in heated discussions sometimes overheard by neighbors, 'never told me to be a lawyer, but he turned me into one.'"

But Marshall did not choose the law right off. After a solid but not superior performance in high school—although he did excel in debating—Marshall, as had Aubrey, went to Lincoln College in Oxford, Pennsylvania, where all the

Young Thurgood Marshall.

students were black and all the professors were white. His mother hoped he would become a dentist. Once again, he was a promising student and a skilled debater, but he often seemed content to float through on talent alone. As he approached his senior year, however, Marshall realized how much he enjoyed argument, public speaking, and interacting directly with people, and also how committed he was to pursuing equal rights for his people. From there, it was a short road to decide to pursue the law. His attitude toward his studies changed, and he graduated with honors.

Ordinarily, he would have chosen the University of Maryland Law School, where his qualifications were more than sufficient to get him admitted. But Maryland was all white, and the state had no black law schools. But Washington, DC, was only an hour away by train, and Howard University's law school had developed a reputation for excellence that matched Marshall's desire for excellence. He applied, was accepted, and, in a meeting that would change American history, went off to study with Charlie Houston.

It was as if each of them had been on a quest to meet the other. For Marshall, Houston was exactly the combination of high intellect, dedication to social justice, commitment to hard work, and precise application of the law that he needed to become an attorney who could win big cases against white adversaries. He soon became the best student in his class and would often remain at Howard until midnight, working in the law library, before taking the train home, grabbing a few hours' sleep, and then returning early the next morning. For Houston, a brilliant protégé like Marshall was proof that segregation and racial discrimination in all forms could be successfully attacked in the courts, and that African American lawyers could triumph over white judges in addition to white lawyers.

After graduation, however, Thurgood Marshall did not immediately set out to win fame and fortune prosecuting equal rights cases before the Supreme Court. As had Charles Houston before him, he set himself up in local practice, taking the cases of African Americans who had few other legal options. And scant money to pay, because in 1934, when Marshall began, the Great Depression was raging and people of color, who even in good times were pushed to the bottom of the economic ladder, had suffered more than almost any other group. In his first year, Marshall made barely enough money to afford to live. He did, however, gain a reputation as a fine lawyer, willing to work diligently and with passion for little or no money. When the NAACP named Charles Houston to be its legal counsel, Houston went out and hired his former star student.

Houston's plan for attacking segregation in graduate schools had not changed, but putting it into practice had turned out to be more difficult than he anticipated. He had to find just the right plaintiff—the person bringing the lawsuit—or the challenge would fail. Regardless of whatever discrimination might be present, if the school could make the case that the person seeking admission was not qualified, no judge would order him or her admitted. Houston had experienced that failure when he sued to gain admission for Thomas Hocutt to a school of pharmacy and Hocutt had made such a poor witness that the court ruled against him.

But soon, Marshall came across Donald Murray, a highly qualified African American who was trying to be admitted to the very University of Maryland Law School that Marshall himself had not been able to attend. Marshall took the case. It would be heard in Maryland state court, rather than federal court, but a victory would be an excellent beginning.

It would not be easy, of course. Marshall would be suing an all-white school before all-white judges, opposed by all-white counsel. But he had trained for this very sort of contest. During the summers of his college years, Marshall had followed his father and worked first as a steward on the B&O Railroad and then as a waiter at the country club. The experience turned out to gain Marshall more than money—by interacting with wealthy white customers, he got a real sense of how they thought, and how they would react to a black man who insisted on behaving as their equal. That training would pay dividends for Marshall's entire career. "Marshall was a rare combination in terms of personality. He was someone both unpretentious and humble—he didn't

(From left) Thurgood Marshall, Donald Murray, and
Charles H. Houston during court proceedings, circa 1935.

tout his own accomplishments—and gregarious, sharp-witted, loud, and funny. He was equally quick to give others credit as to share a bourbon, an off-color joke, and a story or two. In the courtroom, he made his case with facts, the law, and the Constitution in a frank manner, neither alienating juries, Southern judges, nor opposing counsels, with whom he generally got along."

Donald Murray had been one of nine African Americans who had applied and been rejected by the University of Maryland Law School. He was twenty years old, a graduate of Amherst College, and came from a prominent family. Although he had been rejected out of hand by the university's president, Raymond Pearson, with a series of insulting notes, Maryland had no law mandating segregation in its colleges and graduate schools. It was merely "custom" and "policy."

When *Murray v. Pearson* went to trial in a Maryland court, Charles Houston stepped in as lead lawyer. In a series of brilliant witness examinations, he demolished Maryland's defense. To Raymond Pearson's claim that black students could receive substantially the same quality of instruction at Princess Anne Academy, the "Negro college," Houston asked if the faculty had a similar number of professors with advanced degrees—it did not—and if the physical facilities were even remotely comparable—they were not. He next asked the dean of the university law school how black students could get training in the laws of Maryland in any institution that African Americans could attend, including Howard University Law School. The dean admitted they could not. By the time Houston had completed his questioning, there was no doubt at all that, at least for law students in Maryland, separate was most certainly not equal.

From there, Thurgood Marshall took over. His job was to establish for the court that, in the face of *Plessy* and *Gong Lum*, there would be no constitutional issue if the State of Maryland was required to either admit Donald Murray to the university law school or establish a separate—and equal—law school for students of color. *Plessy*, he told the judge, did not apply because there was no equality; nor did *Gong Lum* because there was no black law school for Donald Murray to attend.

The judge agreed. He ordered Donald Murray admitted to the University of Maryland Law School. When the state appealed to the Maryland Supreme Court, the decision was upheld. In what must have been a minor disappointment to Houston and Marshall, the state chose to accept the decision and not appeal to the United States Supreme Court, where a victory would have had application in every state in the Union. Still, there was no diminishing the magnitude of the achievement. Donald Murray graduated in 1938 and went on to practice law in Baltimore, including in a number of civil rights cases for the NAACP, until he retired in 1971.

CHAPTER
11

Setbacks

WHEN DONALD MURRAY walked into a classroom at the University of Maryland Law School, where he received, in his words, "uniformly kind and courteous treatment from the faculty," school segregation had suffered its first defeat. But following up on the victory would not be easy.

The NAACP was overwhelmed. They had been in the forefront of an anti-lynching campaign, continued to be active in the effort to secure voting rights for African Americans, and were involved in a number of criminal cases where black men had been unjustly accused of rape or murder and would certainly have been executed without energetic, committed outside legal assistance. Then there was the problem of having enough money to support these activities. Walter White was an excellent fund-raiser, but still the NAACP was consistently struggling to meet its expenses.

In addition, a successful lawsuit needed a suitable plaintiff, and these were not easy to come by. Houston thought he had one when, in 1935, Lloyd Gaines, "president of his senior class, an honors graduate in history and a skilled debater" from Missouri's all-black Lincoln University, was refused admission to the University of Missouri Law School. Although Missouri offered to pay Gaines's tuition at an out-of-state school, Gaines, like Donald Murray, wanted to practice law in his home state and therefore needed training in Missouri law. He would not have gotten it in another state. After losing in state court, using *Murray* as a precedent, Charles Houston and Thurgood Marshall appealed to the United States Supreme Court.

They won what seemed to be a stunning victory. On December 12, 1938, the Court ruled 6–2 that Missouri must open a law school at Lincoln the equal of the university's law school, or admit Lloyd Gaines to the all-white facility. The Court's ruling at first seemed to be one of the most important equal rights cases in history, the first time a state had ever been held accountable for both parts of the *Plessy* ruling. The "equal" in "separate but equal" could now be applied across the nation.

But Missouri was not ready to quit. Rather than admit Gaines, in January 1939, the state legislature voted to open a law school at Lincoln University, although it would lack both the facilities and the faculty of the state university. It would, in fact, be housed in what had been a beauty school. Houston immediately announced his intention to go back to the Supreme Court. Gaines had by that time earned a master's degree in economics at the University of Michigan. The Supreme Court agreed to rehear the case, and Houston and Marshall prepared with great enthusiasm.

Then Lloyd Gaines disappeared.

In Chicago, on the evening of March 19, 1939, with a cold rain pelting down, filling the streets with slush, Gaines told a friend he needed to buy stamps, even though all the post offices were closed. He left his apartment house and did not return. Although some family members thought he had been kidnapped and murdered, Gaines had been behaving oddly for months, and most people believed that, for reasons of his own, Lloyd Gaines had simply left.

With Gaines no longer available, Missouri asked that the case be dismissed. The NAACP was in no position to object. And so a powerful precedent was lost. Lloyd Gaines was never heard from again. In 2006, the University of Missouri awarded him an honorary law degree.

In July 1938, as he and Marshall were preparing to argue the first Gaines case before the Supreme Court, Charles Houston resigned as legal counsel of the NAACP. He was exhausted, ground down by an inhuman workload and a tubercular condition that had plagued him since his army days. In addition, although he and Walter White shared the same goals, their styles were very different and it seemed best for everyone if Houston moved back to Washington. He remained on the Gaines case and would be active in equal rights cases for the rest of his life but only as a private lawyer.

To take his place—and become the most important black lawyer in the United States—the NAACP chose thirty-year-old Thurgood Marshall. Two years later, Marshall would gain even more power. The NAACP could not accept tax-deductible gifts because it was registered as a lobbying association, a group that openly attempted to persuade congressmen to support certain legislation, such as the anti-lynching bill. To get around that prohibition, in 1940, the NAACP established a separate organization, the Legal Defense and Educational Fund, which would handle its lawsuits and other legal activities. Thurgood Marshall was named executive director of what became known as the LDF, a title he would hold until 1961.

Although in his new position, Marshall would have welcomed another ideal plaintiff to test racial segregation in graduate schools, he simply lacked the time to seek one out. He was doing the work of two, even three people. He had, for example, spent an enormous amount of time in Maryland and then in Virginia, securing equal pay for black teachers. He had also fought attempts by white Southern

Thurgood Marshall around the time he replaced Charles Houston as the NAACP's legal counsel.

Democrats to ensure that African Americans could continue to be denied the right to vote, or if they got to the ballot box, that their votes would have no meaning. In this and other equal rights initiatives in the South, Marshall and the NAACP got no help from the federal government. White, racist Democrats, especially in the Senate, exerted enormous influence in Congress, and President Franklin Roosevelt needed their support to push through his New

Deal programs, most of which were written specifically to exclude black people. (For example, minimum wage laws excluded agricultural and domestic workers, two areas in which African American labor was concentrated.)

To push the equal rights initiatives forward, to make greater progress in ending legal segregation in schools and elsewhere, the NAACP was going to need more than the occasional victory—it would need a change in the way the nation viewed black people, and even a change in the way many black people viewed themselves.

Change that would begin on the battlefield and the ball field.

CHAPTER 12

No Turning Back

BEFORE THE JAPANESE attack on Pearl Harbor on December 7, 1941, fewer than four thousand African Americans were serving in the racially segregated armed forces, and almost all of these were cooks, orderlies, or held menial jobs of other sorts. Only twelve were officers. During the next four years, more than one million black Americans would serve in the US Army, Navy, Air Force, Marines, and Coast Guard. Those one million men and women would not only shatter the myth that "Negroes would not fight," but were also the beginnings of an awakening of consciousness among people of color themselves, a determination to accept nothing less than full equality under the law.

That process began on Pearl Harbor Day itself. During the attack on the battleship USS *West Virginia*, a mess attendant named Doris "Dorie" Miller, who had been doing laundry, came on deck and risked his life helping to move the wounded to safety. He tried to assist the *West Virginia's* captain, Mervyn Bennion, but the commander would not leave his post and died on the bridge. Miller then found an unmanned antiaircraft machine gun and, although he had never been trained to use it, fired at the oncoming Japanese planes, possibly downing one, before being ordered to abandon ship. Once in the water, he again helped the wounded. For his bravery under fire, Dorie Miller was awarded the Navy Cross, the first ever given to an African American. On May 27, 1942, Admiral Chester Nimitz personally pinned the medal to Miller's uniform on the deck of the aircraft carrier USS *Enterprise*. Eighteen months later, Dorie Miller was dead, killed when his ship was torpedoed by a Japanese submarine near the Gilbert Islands in the central Pacific Ocean. On January 20, 2020, Martin Luther King Day, Acting Secretary of the Navy Thomas Modly announced that a new aircraft carrier would be named the USS *Doris Miller*, the first aircraft carrier to be named for an African American and also the first for an enlisted man.

Dorie Miller in many ways exemplified the experience of African Americans serving in the armed forces during World War II. Almost all began in the sort of lower-level jobs Miller was forced into but, as the war progressed, participated more and more in combat, earning praise and respect from officers, many of whom were from the Jim Crow South.

Their stories were reported in newspapers and magazines

as well, and many white Americans who thought sports heroes, such as heavyweight champion Joe Louis and the brilliant Olympian Jesse Owens, were rare exceptions, came to understand that many black men and women deserved their admiration. They read of the more than 1,700 black soldiers who helped storm the beaches of Normandy on D-Day, and the all–African American 761st Tank Battalion, the Black Panthers, which fought its way through France with General George S. Patton's vaunted Third Army and were credited with capturing thirty major towns in France, Belgium, and Germany.

And then, of course, there was the 332nd Fighter Group, the famed Tuskegee Airmen, who flew more than fifteen thousand sorties and saw sixty-six of their number killed in combat. In 1945, the army air corps produced a documentary depicting pilot training and the combat operations of the 332nd, *Wings for This Man*, which ended with the narrator saying, "You don't judge a man by the

Lieutenant General George Patton awards the Silver Star to Private Ernest A. Jenkins.

The 761st Tank Battalion.

shape of his nose or the color of his skin." That narrator was US Army Air Corps Captain Ronald Reagan.

But heroism in combat and propaganda films did not put an end to American racism. The Tuskegee Airmen and tank gunners of the 761st still could not be served a meal in the same facilities where German prisoners of war were allowed to eat. As in the First World War, for the hundreds of thousands of black soldiers who would be stationed in Europe, the contrast could not have been more striking. They had suddenly been thrown into cultures where not only were they not thought to be inferior but were often treated as being special because of the color of their skin. In one English town, when US military authorities demanded that the pubs impose a color bar, the landlords responded with signs that read: BLACK TROOPS ONLY.

After the experience of being treated as equals—and fighting as equals—in Europe, it was nearly impossible that these and other black Americans would meekly accept Jim Crow subservience once the conflict ended. One soldier, Roscoe Pickett, recalled that by serving in the army, he learned an important fact about himself. "I knew then that I wasn't going to go back on the farm. I knew that I was going to go to college somewhere. That's the thing that changed my life. I knew that a black man could do things other than mess around plowing with an ox, messing around cutting cross-ties. That's the thing that changed me." Another veteran, Wilford Strange, in the 2013 documentary *Choc'late Soldiers from the USA*, which "tells the story of 140,000 Black American soldiers and thousands of British civilians who crossed a racial divide to forge an unexpected bond," said, "I think the impact these soldiers had by volunteering was the initiation of the Civil Rights movement, 'cause these soldiers were never going back to be discriminated against again. None of us were." When they returned home, black military veterans joined the NAACP by the thousands and began new chapters, mostly in the segregated South.

And in the home they returned to, battles of a different sort were raging.

Even before the United States entered the conflict, civil rights activity had stepped up to a level not seen since Reconstruction. Months before Pearl Harbor, defense companies had hired hundreds of thousands of white workers, in case the United States was drawn into the war. In March 1941, A. Philip Randolph, president of the Brotherhood of Sleeping Car Porters, wrote to Walter White at the NAACP, and said that "something drastic has got to be done to shake official Washington and the white industrialists and labor forces of America to the realization of the fact that Negroes mean business about getting their rights as American citizens under national defense." He proposed a mass march on Washington to protest unfair hiring practices.

Such a protest was a threat that President Roosevelt could

not ignore. A march on Washington could well result in a bloody riot, which would be covered by news outlets across the globe. The United States had been telling the world that "the land of the free" opposed the fascism of Hitler's Germany and Mussolini's Italy, but both dictators pointed to racism and segregation in the United States as proof that America was no better than they were. For the fascists, and even the communists in Joseph Stalin's Russia, a race riot in the nation's capital would be a propaganda triumph.

Randolph and White were called to the White House in June 1941 to discuss the problem, and one week later, the president issued an order that forbade hiring discrimination in any defense industry that had received a government contract. To ensure that the order was followed, Roosevelt established the Fair Employment Practices Committee. As a result, tens of thousands of African Americans would be hired at defense plants at good pay.

African American leaders sensed an opening and kept up the pressure. In early 1942, with the United States now at war, the *Pittsburgh Courier*, one of the nation's most important black newspapers, launched a drive against fascism overseas and against racism at home. "We, as colored Americans are determined to protect our country, our form of government and the freedoms which we cherish for ourselves and the rest of the world, therefore we have adopted the Double 'V' war cry—victory over our enemies at home and victory over our enemies on the battlefields abroad. Thus in our fight for freedom we wage a two-pronged attack against our enslavers at home and those abroad who will enslave us. WE HAVE A STAKE IN THIS FIGHT . . . WE ARE AMERICANS, TOO!"

The Double V Campaign was soon adopted by African Americans across America. Black Americans, both in the military and those working in defense plants, had moved into mainstream society despite all efforts by segregationists to hold them back. But white rage increased as well, especially among those who watched jobs they thought should be theirs going to black workers, or homes they thought should be theirs occupied by black families.

Sometimes that rage boiled over. In June 1943, while hundreds of thousands of black soldiers were either risking their lives in Europe and the Pacific or preparing to, twenty-five African Americans were murdered in a massive race riot in Detroit.

The end of the war brought additional challenges, especially in the South, where African Americans who had served their country became special targets. So much did black soldiers enrage white supremacists that they were advised not to wear their uniforms once they got home. It did not always matter. In February 1946, Isaac Woodard, a black veteran of World War II, was attacked and blinded by policemen in Aiken, South Carolina. No one was punished or arrested.

That July, two other black veterans and their wives were dragged from their car near Monroe, Georgia, by a white mob. Sixty bullets were pumped into their bodies. This time, however, rather than allow what came to be known as the Moore's Ford lynchings to simply become one more anonymous racial barbarity,

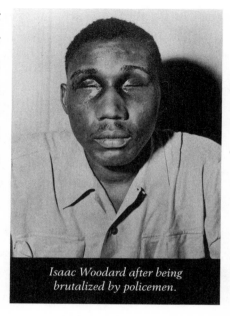

Isaac Woodard after being brutalized by policemen.

President Harry S. Truman instructed the Justice Department to "proceed with all its resources to investigate the atrocity and other crimes of oppression so as to ascertain if any Federal statute can be applied." The FBI investigated and offered rewards, but the crime was never solved. (It was reopened in the 1990s, but the FBI could not gather enough evidence against their prime suspects to make an arrest.)

Nonetheless, the publicity the case created allowed African American leaders to step up pressure on the government to take action to ensure equal treatment and basic protections for their people. In response, later that year, President Truman empanelled the President's Committee on Civil Rights. In October 1947, the committee issued its report *To*

Secure These Rights, which condemned segregation in American society, especially in the armed forces. It recommended action by both Congress and the president "to end immediately all discrimination and segregation based on race, color, creed or national origin in all branches of the Armed Services."

President Harry S. Truman.

Early the next year, President Truman did just that. Rather than wait for Congress, which was still largely dominated by racist senators and representatives from the South, he issued an executive order ending segregation in the military and instructed heads of the armed forces, which also contained a large number of senior white segregationist officers, to immediately begin to develop plans for integrating America's military.

Racial barriers were beginning to break down in other areas, none more important than in what was legitimately called the country's national pastime. In 1946, Brooklyn Dodger owner Branch Rickey shocked and horrified millions of baseball fans by signing Jackie Robinson to play in the Dodger organization. Robinson, the grandson of a Georgia slave, was a superb athlete, a star in football, baseball, basketball, and track at UCLA. He was also proud, smart, brave, and iron-willed.

In 1941, Robinson had joined the army and was commissioned as a lieutenant in the 761st Tank Battalion. But he was court-martialed when he refused to move to the back of a bus at Camp Hood in Texas. "I was aware of the fact that recently [heavyweight champion] Joe Louis and [boxer Sugar] Ray Robinson had refused to move to the backs of buses in the South. The resulting publicity had caused the Army to put out regulations barring racial discrimination on any vehicle operating on an Army post. Knowing about these regulations, I had no intention of being intimidated into moving to the back of the bus." The charges were dropped when the white commanding officer refused to sign the official papers. Robinson was transferred to another unit, where he served out his time without having the chance to fight in Europe.

But it was Robinson's behavior during the court-martial proceedings that convinced Dodger owner Branch Rickey that he had found what he was looking for. "A man of principle. A moral man . . . I had to get a man who could carry the burden on the field. I needed a man to carry the badge of martyrdom."

After a year playing for the Dodger farm team in Montreal, Canada, where segregation did not exist—and he was the league's Most Valuable Player—Robinson joined the Dodgers in 1947. To the anger and dismay of those who saw the purity of the game defiled, Robinson was an immediate star. He led the Dodgers to the National League pennant, was Rookie of the Year, and finished fifth in the voting for Most Valuable Player. The Dodgers drew 1.8 million paying customers, the largest attendance in their history. Robinson's appeal went beyond Brooklyn. Attendance records were set around the league as both black and white baseball fans and curiosity seekers flooded stadiums to see him play. With dollars flowing into their coffers, team owners, who had at first resisted integrating the sacred sport of baseball, decided it

Jackie Robinson stealing home in the 1955 World Series.

*The all–African American outfield of the New York Giants.
From left: Monte Irvin, Willie Mays, and Hank Thompson.*

wasn't such a bad idea after all. Jackie Robinson would eventually be named to the All Star team six times, be named Most Valuable Player in 1949, and be inducted into baseball's Hall of Fame. To this day, his number, 42, is the only one retired by every team in Major League Baseball.

In July of that same year, Cleveland Indians owner Bill Veeck signed center fielder Larry Doby, the first African American to play in the American League. Doby, while far less well known than Robinson, was also a superb player, voted to the All Star team seven times, and eventually to the Hall of Fame. Other great players followed soon afterward, including Hall of Famers Roy Campanella; Monte Irvin; the ageless Satchel Paige; and, in 1951, a man many still consider to be the greatest all-around player in history, Willie Mays. That year, Mays joined Irvin and Hank Thompson in an all-black outfield for the National League champion New York Giants.

By the early 1950s, all three of the nation's major sports boasted African American stars. White Americans went from outrage to a thirst to see these men play, and sports stadiums became integrated as a result. When mixed race teams traveled, most would eventually stay only in hotels that treated all the players the same, thereby integrating any number of those facilities as well. Local restaurants followed. Although enormous resistance to African Americans on sports teams remained, the trend was unstoppable. Fans preferred integrated teams that won to all-white teams that did not.

To all but the most die-hard white supremacist, it was clear that segregation in other areas of American life, schools for example, was ripe to be toppled. No one thought the job would be easy, and it would take great courage from both black and white Americans, but after Dorie Miller, Jackie Robinson, the Tuskegee Airmen, and thousands of others, the example of that courage had been put forth for all to see.

CHAPTER 13

Renewing the Attack

LEGAL CHALLENGES TO segregation slowed during the war but did not end. Although not every lawsuit resulted in a victory, there was a definite trend to begin to see segregation in a new light. In one case, *Morgan v. Virginia*, the Court accepted an unusual tactic by William Hastie and Thurgood Marshall to overturn a long-standing tradition of segregation on buses, trains, and boats that traveled across two or more states.

On July 16, 1944, an African American woman, Irene Morgan, who was employed in a defense plant, boarded a Greyhound bus in Virginia to return home to Baltimore. She had been recuperating at her mother's home after a miscarriage and was still quite weak. The bus was crowded, but she found a seat in the "colored" section at the back. By the time a young white couple boarded the bus farther up the line, all the seats in the white section were full. The bus driver told Morgan to surrender her seat. Morgan refused.

The driver, furious that a black woman had refused his order, drove to the local jail, where a sheriff's deputy came aboard. He handed Morgan an arrest warrant. She tore it up and tossed it out the bus window. One of the officers then swore at her and tried to grab her arm to physically remove her from the bus.

As Morgan said later, "He touched me. That's when I kicked him in a very bad place. He hobbled off, and another one came on. He was trying to put his hands on me to get me off. I was going to bite him, but he was dirty, so I clawed him instead. I ripped his shirt. We were both pulling at each other. He said he'd use his nightstick. I said, 'We'll whip each other.'"

Irene Morgan was eventually dragged off the bus and taken to jail for resisting arrest and violating Virginia's segregation law, which said that people of color had to yield seats to whites. She was released when her mother posted $500 bail, but she had to pay a $100 fine after she pleaded guilty to resisting arrest. She refused to pay the $10 fine for violating the segregation law, however. It would be $10 Virginia wished it had written off.

This was precisely the sort of case the LDF was looking for—a challenge to equal rights that would have wide impact, brought by an admirable and sympathetic plaintiff.

The Supreme Court had ruled on a number of similar cases in the 1880s and 1890s and had always found an excuse to rule in favor of segregation. So Marshall and Hastie needed to find a way for the Court to go back on those earlier rulings without appearing to directly overrule them. The justices were certainly not ready to go *that* far. So the two lawyers for the NAACP did not bring the case on Fourteenth Amendment grounds—equal protection of the laws—but rather argued that according to Article I, Section 8 of the Constitution, only Congress has the power "to regulate commerce with foreign nations, and among the several states." Virginia, therefore, had no power to enforce segregated seating on any public conveyance traveling between states.

Fifty years earlier, Marshall and Hastie would certainly have lost. This time they won. With only one dissent, the Court ruled in favor of the black woman passenger and against the state of Virginia. "It seems clear to us," wrote Justice Stanley Reed, "that seating arrangements for the different races in interstate motor travel require a single, uniform rule to promote and protect national travel. Consequently, we hold the Virginia statute in controversy invalid." While not ruling on segregation itself, forcing white people to at least legally accept having black neighbors on interstate travel was one more small step to outlawing segregation altogether.

Two years later, the NAACP scored another major victory—and erased another adverse decision. J. D. and Ethel

Morgan Vs. State of Virginia

Case to be Supreme Court Hot Potato

1-26-46 4x

By Richard Dier

At last a clear case to test the jim-crow travel laws of Southern states which segregate interstate passengers on interstate carriers before the U.S. Supreme Court! The case, which is the first real test to be made of a law which liberates against colored passengers in a number of Southern states, involves Mrs. Irene A. Morgan of 550 W. 144th St., New York City.

She was arrested in Saluda, Va., and charged with violation of the Virginia statute requiring segregation of passengers.

The incident took place July 16, 1944, when Mrs. Morgan was a passenger on a Greyhound Bus from Gloucester County, Va., to Baltimore, Md.

Refused to Move

She refused to give up her seat to a white couple at a bus stop in Saluda. Arrested and forced to post $500 bail for her release, she was convicted and fined on Oct. 18, 1944, in the Circuit Court of Middlesex County.

Her case was promptly appealed to the Supreme Court of Virginia on a writ of error.

On June 6, 1945, the Circuit Court's judgment was upheld by the Supreme Court of Virginia on the grounds that the Virginia jim-crow statute was constitutional and applied to interstate as well as local passengers.

A motion for rehearing was filed and subsequently denied by the Supreme Court in September.

Not on Calendar Yet

Chief Justice Harlan F. Stone of the U.S. Supreme Court signed an order, Nov. 19, 1945, allowing her to appeal the judgment of the Supreme Court of Virginia. The U.S. Supreme Court has not placed the case on the calendar yet.

In an exclusive AFRO interview, Mrs. Morgan described the incident. She had been visiting her mother in Gloucester County, following an operation she had undergone in Baltimore.

She was returning to Baltimore for further medical treatment. She boarded a Greyhound Bus at 10 a.m. Sunday, July 16, 1944.

"The bus was quite crowded and there were a lot of people standing," Mrs. Morgan explained.

Ordered to Move

"A colored woman, who was seated, noticed I was tired and offered to let me sit on her lap. I accepted this offer because I was not feeling well, and sat on her lap for a few minutes in the rear of the bus.

"As the bus pulled into a stop in Saluda, a passenger vacated a seat, third from the rear, and I took it. A young colored woman with a baby in her arms sat next to me.

"It was around 11 a.m. now.

Suddenly, the white bus driver came over and told us we would have to give up our seats to a young white couple who just got on the bus.

"'You'll have to get up and give your seats to these people,' he demanded.

"I told him I wouldn't mind exchanging seats with white people told me again to get up and stand."

Returns with Policemen

Mrs. Morgan said the driver got off the bus and returned with two white police officers.

They came over to her, and the driver said colored were to be seated when all whites were seated. One officer asked, "Are you gonna get up or not?"

"The officers said they had a warrant for me," Mrs. Morgan continued. "I asked them what the warrant was for. They both grabbed hold of me, each one tugging at one of my arms, and

forced me out of my seat and out of the bus.

"When I told them they were hurting my arms, one said, 'Wait till I get you to jail; I'll beat your head with a stick.'"

The names of the two men were Bristol and Segar.

"The jail was across the street from the Saluda bus station. They locked me up until 5:30 p.m. A minister, the Rev. Mr. Gale, whom I knew, got word to my mother back in Gloucester County. She rushed to the jail and posted a $500 bond before I was released."

Her arms were torn to pieces, Mrs. Morgan said, and treatment involved considerable medical expenses.

Dr. Tinsley, president of the Virginia State Conference of the NAACP, Spotswood Robinson III of Howard University and Thurgood Marshall of the NAACP took over her case.

On Oct. 18, 1944, she was convicted on two charges; she was fined $100 for resisting an officer, and $10 for violation of the State jim-crow law. She paid the $100 fine on the first charge, but appealed the second one.

"Means a Lot"

"This case means a lot to me," she told the AFRO, "because my family and I travel frequently to Virginia to visit my mother. My two children go there for summer vacations, and we all want to be able to travel without jim-crow restrictions."

Mrs. Morgan, who is 28, is intelligent and pretty. She is married and lives with her husband, Sherwood, and family in a large apartment house of which he is superintendent.

They have two children, a boy of 5 and a girl of 3.

Born in Baltimore, Mrs. Morgan was educated in the public and high schools there and attended business school in New York.

She works in Manhattan, caring for an invalid. She has been living in New York since last September.

Mrs. Irene Morgan, who was arrested and charged with violation of the Virginia statute requiring segregation of passengers. The Supreme Court of Virginia upheld the lower court decision. Mrs. Morgan has appealed to the U.S. Supreme Court.

OPEN WIDE!

Sen. Claude Pepper's Subcommittee on Health reports on the nation's most recently discovered backlog.

It consists of 238,000,000 needed tooth extractions, 632,000,000 needed fillings, 39,500,000 crowns and bridges, 20,000,000 partial dentures, and 20,000,000 dental disease treatments.

All this was discovered, naturally enough, because people just can't seem to learn to keep their big mouths shut.—UNCLE MAT'S MONTHLY LETTER.

A newspaper headline covering Morgan v. Virginia.

Lee Shelley, both African American, bought a house in St. Louis, Missouri, in a neighborhood that had drafted a private restrictive covenant—although no one had told the Shelleys. This was the very sort of arrangement the Court had approved in *Corrigan v. Buckley*. Louis Kraemer, a white homeowner who lived half a mile away, sued to prevent the Shelleys from moving into their new home. Missouri state courts ruled for Kraemer because the arrangement was not a state law, but simply an agreement among private property owners.

The LDF took the case and Charles Houston participated as well, although only as a lawyer in private practice. They appealed to the Supreme Court, this time on the same Fourteenth Amendment grounds—denial of "equal protection of the laws"—that Marshall had avoided in *Morgan v. Virginia*. As it had in *Morgan*, the Court ruled for the black plaintiff but avoided ruling on segregation itself. The vote was 6–0. Three justices were forced to recuse themselves—not participate—because they lived in neighborhoods with restrictive covenants. The opinion was an excellent example of justices jumping through legal hoops in order to end up with the decision they want.

The Court acknowledged that the Fourteenth Amendment applies to states alone and not to private individuals. Private individuals are allowed to discriminate in any way they like, be it on the basis of race, religion, or on any other grounds.

And so, the restrictive covenant was legal. BUT, the state cannot interfere with any person's right to buy, sell, lease, or donate property because of the race of the owner or the person who acquires it. And courts are part of the states. So, while the covenant might technically be legal, it could not be enforced by state courts. That meant that even though the Shelleys' purchase might have violated the covenant, there was nothing anyone else in the neighborhood could do about it. The covenant was a dead letter. Anyone willing to sell to a black person or family could not be prevented from doing so.

CHAPTER 14

A School of One's Own

S CHOOL SEGREGATION WAS still the LDF's main focus, and graduate and professional schools the first area of attack. As always, finding just the right plaintiff was one of the major challenges, and Marshall, as the 1940s drew to a close, was fortunate to have located two.

The first was Heman Sweatt. However unusual his name, his qualifications were excellent. Born in Houston, Texas, in 1912, the son of a school principal, Sweatt graduated from an all-black Texas college and then taught at a segregated grade school, where he was also acting principal. Thinking of perhaps becoming a doctor, he spent two semesters studying biology at the University of Michigan, before changing his mind and returning home. He worked as a mailman to earn money, married his high school sweetheart, and bought a small house.

His fellow postal workers chose him to head their local

union chapter, where Sweatt used that position to challenge discriminatory practices in the post office. To become a supervisor, a postal worker first had to work as a clerk, but black employees were not allowed to fill those positions. Sweatt initiated a legal challenge and, while working with a local black lawyer, decided to become a lawyer himself.

African American lawyers in Texas were an almost nonexistent species. In 1940, there were 7,570 white lawyers registered in the state; the number of black lawyers was *22*. One of the reasons the number was so low was that there was no law school in the state in which they could acquire the proper training. Like Donald Murray in Maryland, the only way a Texas African American could study law was to leave the state, and therefore not be schooled in Texas law. The University of Texas Law School in Austin was excellent but would not admit black students. The state, as did Missouri in the Lloyd Gaines case, had established a scholarship program for black students who wished to study in fields not offered at black state colleges, but these would not help students become Texas lawyers. As a result, almost all of the scholarship applicants chose to study medicine, for which training was not specific to each state.

In early 1946, with the support of the Texas NAACP, Heman Sweatt applied for admission to the University of Texas Law School, the first person of color ever to do so. He was rejected. Sweatt sued the law school and the president of the university, Theophilus Painter, to gain admission. A local judge agreed that Sweatt was qualified for admission, but he allowed the state six months to establish a law school for black students equal to that available for whites.

The state moved quickly to set up a law school at Prairie View University, the only black college in Texas that could offer graduate degrees. They "secured the law offices and part of the library of a Negro attorney in Houston who was to serve as dean and teacher. The physical facilities consisted of only three rooms, two of which lacked chairs and desks, and none of which had bookshelves." University representatives told Heman Sweatt that he could now study to be a lawyer in the state of Texas.

Twenty years earlier, white authorities in Texas could have congratulated themselves for the clever and inexpensive solution they had devised to solve an annoying problem, but times had changed. When Sweatt declined to take courses at what was a law school in name only and instead announced his intention to continue his legal challenges, Texas state legislators were forced to declare their intention to create a "first class" university for black students. They allocated $2 million to build and staff it, $100,000 of which would go to an "interim" law school.

The university rented three basement rooms in an office building just across from the state capitol in Austin, assigned three first-year faculty members at the white law school to teach part-time, and stocked a library of ten thousand old books—the white law school had three to four times that many, and they were up to date. They then told Sweatt he was welcome to register for classes, which were to begin in March 1947.

He declined. Thurgood Marshall, who led Sweatt's legal team, had no intention of settling for anything less than full equality, and full equality meant the white law school in Austin. (As with Donald Murray in Maryland, white students supported Sweatt's admission and had even held a rally on his behalf.) Marshall went back to court, lost, as expected in Texas, and then took the case to Washington. On April 4, 1950, armed with testimony from law school deans, lawyers, and professors that the facility made available to Heman Sweatt was inferior in every way to the white law school, Marshall told the justices that the only way true equality could be achieved—and the conditions of *Plessy* upheld—was for Heman Sweatt to enroll at the University of Texas Law School.

But Marshall had another card to play. Just before he presented Sweatt's case before the Court, Marshall had appeared with another NAACP attorney, Robert L. Carter, to argue for the second of their plaintiffs, sixty-eight-year-old George McLaurin.

McLaurin, who held a master's degree, wished to enter the doctoral program in education at the University of

Oklahoma. His application was rejected. With the help of the NAACP, McLaurin filed a complaint accusing university authorities of violating his Fourteenth Amendment right of equal protection of the laws. A federal district court agreed that Oklahoma "had a Constitutional duty to provide him with the education he sought as soon as it provided that education for applicants of any other group." So white leaders devised a particularly humiliating plan, wherein McLaurin could attend classes but had to sit alone at a desk in a tiny anteroom outside the classroom, or in the hall, and observe the professor through an open door. He was also required "to sit at a designated desk on the mezzanine floor of the library, but not to use the desks in the regular reading room; and to sit at a designated table and to eat at a different time from the other students in the school cafeteria."

When the NAACP filed suit once more, this time to remove conditions under which George McLaurin was treated as if he were the carrier of a communicable disease, the university changed the rules once more but not much for the better. He was allowed into the classroom, but the section in which he sat—one desk—was surrounded by a rail with a sign that read, RESERVED FOR COLORED. He could use the main floor of the library but had to sit at a special table, and eat in the cafeteria at the same time as other students, but again, only at a special table.

So the NAACP went back to the Supreme Court.

George McLaurin sitting separate from the white students in his class at the University of Oklahoma, 1948.

Although once more they did not directly challenge *Plessy*, they did insist that *any* such separation as the university was trying to force on George McLaurin was by definition inequality. The justices realized full well the significance of such a statement, and no one expected a quick decision.

On April 22, 1950, while Marshall, Carter, and the rest of black America waited for the Court's rulings, Charles Houston died. He was only fifty-four years old. The official cause was a heart attack—and he had suffered another a year earlier—but it would not be a mistake to say that Charlie Houston gave his life for a cause he believed right and just, and had worked to achieve it with such intensity and single-minded dedication that his body simply gave out. But not his spirit. That was with him until the moment he died. There are many heroes in the struggle for equal rights, but none cast a larger shadow than Charles Hamilton Houston.

Houston was thus not at the Court to see a major milestone in his life's quest achieved. Both decisions came down the same day, June 5, 1950; both were unanimous; and both opinions were written by Chief Justice Fred M. Vinson. In *Sweatt*, he wrote, "The legal education offered petitioner is not substantially equal to that which he would receive if admitted to the University of Texas Law School, and the Equal Protection Clause of the Fourteenth Amendment requires that he be admitted to the University of Texas Law School." And in *McLaurin*, "The restrictions imposed upon appellant impair and inhibit his ability to study, to engage in discussions and exchange views with other students, and, in general, to learn his profession . . . Having been admitted to a state supported graduate school, appellant must receive the same treatment at the hands of the State as students of other races."

Another pillar holding up the rotting temple of segregation had been toppled. An article published one year later,

Heman Sweatt waiting in line to register for classes at the University of Texas Law School in Austin, following his major Supreme Court victory.

in 1951, three years before the Court would rule in *Brown*, summed up the two decisions perfectly and also set the stage for what was to come. Titled "The Beginning of the End of the Separate but Equal Doctrine," its authors wrote, "If the two cases are considered together, what one lacks the other supplies in answering in the affirmative the question whether segregation, at least in regard to the higher educational and professional facilities provided by a State, is unconstitutional . . . The only step remaining for the Court to take, in deciding the question whether there is an equal protection of the laws by the State providing separate facilities to distinct groups, is to hold that, in the very nature of separation of the races there is inequality."

Still, while it might have been the last remaining step, it was the biggest step of all, larger than all the previous steps combined. And the risks in taking that step were enormous. The decisions in *Sweatt* and *McLaurin* had not in any way overruled separate but equal. Just the opposite—they had merely held that the "equal" part was as important as "separate." Segregation still stood as the law of the land. If black Americans lost a direct challenge to *Plessy* in the Supreme Court, separate but equal would be recemented in the law and would undo almost all the progress that had been made during the past quarter century.

CHAPTER 15

The Main Event

IN THE WAKE of *Sweatt* and *McLaurin*, law schools in Louisiana, Virginia, and North Carolina were desegregated. As Nathan Margold had predicted, it was simply too expensive for Jim Crow states to establish genuinely equal facilities. Even more significant was when a state judge in Delaware ruled that the undergraduate facilities at Delaware State College for Negroes were not equal to those at the state university for whites. In Missouri, a state judge ruled that an African American high school student was entitled to take the same aeromechanics course as offered in the white high school. But still, even with these victories, segregation itself remained unchallenged.

For all his seeming bravado, Thurgood Marshall was a cautious man. He and many of his colleagues were not yet ready to attack *Plessy* head-on, but the momentum created by him and a growing roster of excellent young black lawyers, including William Hastie and Robert L. Carter, and young white lawyers, such as Jack Greenberg, made it difficult to go in any other direction.

Outside forces were at work as well. Thanks to an exceedingly brave black minister and an equally brave white judge, the perilous journey from "separate but equal" to "separate is unequal" had already begun.

Clarendon County, South Carolina, was in a marshy, wooded, mosquito-ridden area, halfway between Charleston, on the coast, and the state capital, Columbia, located inland. During the Revolutionary War, it had been the site of the aptly named Battle of Halfway Swamp. In the late 1940s, Clarendon County was poor, even by the standards of the poverty-stricken rural South. But as everywhere else in the region, the black community was much, much poorer than even the lowest class of whites, even though African Americans outnumbered whites by more than two to one. In the Davis Station section of the county, black high school–age children had to walk up to nine miles to get to the crumbling building that passed for the local black high school. White children were bused to their school—more than thirty school buses had been purchased for the task.

One of the rare people of color who, by county standards, was even mildly well off, was Rev. J. A. De Laine, pastor of the Society Hill A.M.E Church. De Laine was even a landowner, one of the very few who was not a tenant on white-owned land. In June 1947, he attended an NAACP meeting in Columbia, where the speaker addressed the lack of school buses for black children and told the audience that the first part of *going* to school was *getting* to school.

In July, just as Jackie Robinson was bringing a new dimension to Major League Baseball and drawing record numbers of paying customers to baseball games throughout the National League, Rev. De Laine instructed Harold Boulware, a local black lawyer, to file a petition from local parents asking that one school bus be purchased for the black high school. The reply came from school board chairman R. W. Elliott, a sawmill operator who had himself not finished high school. "We ain't got no money to buy a bus for your nigger children," he wrote.

Rev. De Laine and Boulware had already been in touch with the NAACP headquarters in New York, asking for help in drawing up a complaint that might be filed in federal court. The complaint was filed in March 1948. The case was dismissed, but still, Rev. De Laine had become a marked man. As everyone in the county knew, white supremacists could murder him and not spend a single day in jail for the crime.

But Rev. De Laine kept on. He wrote in an open letter, "Shall we suffer endless persecution just because we want our children reared in a wholesome atmosphere? What some of us have suffered is nothing short of Nazi persecution."

Clarendon County school for white children.

22 Liberty

He recruited almost two dozen parents equally willing to risk their lives and property by becoming plaintiffs, including Harry Briggs, a navy veteran who worked for a white gas station owner, and his wife, Eliza, a maid at a motel. Both knew they would lose their jobs—at least—if a lawsuit were filed. And they did, as did just about everyone who joined them in the suit.

The hesitancy was on the legal side. Marshall and the LDF were reluctant to take on another "equalization" case, especially one that could be resolved with a single bus. What pushed him forward, what gave Marshall and the LDF the opportunity to make *Briggs v. Elliott* important—really

Harry Briggs stands in front of the Scott's Branch School in Summerton, South Carolina, May 8, 1979. In 1949, Briggs filed a school desegregation lawsuit, seeking equal schools and pay for teachers.

important—was the white federal judge who would hear the case, J. (for Julius) Waties Waring.

What made Judge Waring so irresistible to Marshall was that most South Carolina whites loathed him as a traitor to his race and his class. Little in Waring's background would have given hints of that outcome. Born in 1880, his family had been in Charleston for eight generations, and his father had fought for the Confederacy during the Civil War. He attended school with other children of the elite at Charleston's private University School, then went on to the segregated College of Charleston. Upon graduation, he did not go to law school, but instead apprenticed with one of the city's most prominent white attorneys. He married well, became involved in Democratic Party politics, served for a time as a United States attorney, and then became a partner in a successful law practice. Just after his sixtieth birthday, as a result of his political connections, he was appointed to be a federal district court judge, fully expected to use his position to uphold white privilege.

For his first two years on the bench, he did precisely that. But then, for reasons that were never entirely clear, Waties Waring underwent a radical change. "In 1944, he began handing down decisions equalizing the salaries of black and white teachers, ordering the state to desegregate its law school or create an equal facility for blacks, and rebuffing South Carolina's efforts to salvage its all-white

Democratic primary. The judge's rulings angered white South Carolinians. In addition, his 1945 divorce from his wife of more than thirty years, followed almost immediately by his marriage to Elizabeth Hoffman, a twice-divorced Northern matron, enraged his family and former friends." Waring, with the full support of his new wife, became a crusader for equal rights, and even invited prominent African Americans to his home in a section of Charleston where the only other black faces were on the servants.

Segregationists unsuccessfully sought his impeachment, his home was stoned, and a cross was burned on his lawn. But Waring would not be intimidated. And so, when Thurgood Marshall learned that Waring would sit on *Briggs v. Elliott*, he decided to proceed.

But Waring had a surprise for the NAACP. He did not intend to sit on *Briggs v. Elliott*. Not alone at any rate. What was more, where Marshall wanted to win his case, Waring wanted him to lose it. Waring instructed Marshall that instead of bringing an action on school buses before a single federal judge—him—Marshall should instead challenge segregation as being "unequal *per se*," and go before a three-judge federal appeals court, which included Waring. If, or more likely when, the Clarendon parents lost 2–1, Marshall would then have grounds to appeal to the Supreme Court.

Now forced to attack *Plessy* and segregation, whether they were ready or not, Marshall and Robert Carter were faced with the problem of just how to do it. Going into court and simply saying that the justices who decided *Plessy* did so because of race prejudice would not do. They needed a strategy that would imply that while the *Plessy* reasoning might have been acceptable in 1896, new information, a new point of view, made it unacceptable a half century later. They struck on a tactic that made an already risky case riskier—that segregation inflicted permanent psychological damage on black children. To try to prove that, they would rely on the work of a controversial African American social psychologist, Kenneth Clark.

Clark, a professor at City College in New York, and his wife, Mamie, also a psychologist, had pioneered an experimental technique called "doll tests" to determine self-esteem in black children. The Clarks placed four one-foot-tall, gender-neutral dolls before a young black child, the dolls identical except that two were pink and two were brown. Clark would ask the child, "Give me the doll that is the nice doll" or "Give me the doll that looks like you" or "Give me the doll you like to play with." The Clarks discovered that almost all the black children chose a pink doll. They explained this by asserting that a majority of black children suffered from "self rejection," because of a belief that their race was inferior. Clark agreed to come to Clarendon County, conduct the doll test on local children, and then testify about the results at trial.

The case was heard on May 28, 1951, and as most people expected, the black parents lost 2–1, Judge Waring being the one. In his dissent, Waring wrote, "I am of the opinion that all of the legal guideposts, expert testimony, common sense and reason point unerringly to the conclusion that the system of segregation in education adopted and practiced in the state of South Carolina must go and go now. Segregation is *per se* inequality." The judge's statement, and the Clarks' doll test results—which confirmed that the sixteen black children tested in Clarendon County behaved as had the Clarks' other subjects—were part of the record. With this shaky support, Marshall and Carter headed to the Supreme Court to attack *Plessy v. Ferguson* at its roots.

But they never got the chance. So fearful was South Carolina of losing the case, and segregation along with it, that their lawyers told the justices that the state had instituted a program of improving black schools until they were on a par with white schools and had budgeted more than one million dollars to get it done. Marshall and Carter were not pleased—after all their work, they wanted the case tried on the legality of segregation. But the Court agreed to allow South Carolina the opportunity to implement its new program and told them to report back with their progress in six months.

That was not how things worked out. When next *Briggs v. Elliott* reached the Supreme Court, it had been combined with four other cases, one of which involved Linda Brown, a schoolgirl from Topeka, Kansas. Although *Briggs v. Elliott* was not the named case, the techniques Marshall and Carter employed in South Carolina would be what ultimately destroyed legal segregation in the United States.

But those brave black citizens of Clarendon County paid a heavy price for being the keys to victory. In addition to being fired from their jobs, many had mortgages called in, or were denied the lines of credit they needed to pay their expenses until their crops were harvested. Many white-owned local businesses refused to sell to people of color, no matter which door, front or back, they used. Harry Briggs moved to Florida to be able to work to support his family, and Eliza and the children also eventually left Clarendon County, as did many of the twenty men and women who had agreed to lend their names to the effort.

As for Rev. De Laine—on October 10, 1951, his house was burned to the ground while local white firefighters stood by and watched because the house was twenty feet over the town line. But that was not enough for South Carolina whites. As his son later described, "In '55 my father was given 10 days to leave town or die. Tensions began to heat up. My father, who was a minister, had been forced to take a job at a church outside the county. He was living in Lake City, where this other church was. There was vandalism on the church parsonage. On the seventh day the church was destroyed by arson. On the tenth day there was a delegation, or posse or whatever you want to call it, who paid a visit to the house, and then there was about three rounds of gunfire. On the third round, my father began to shoot back. He allegedly shot some people, though no one was killed. After this happened my father escaped and ended up in New York."

Judge Waring, his life threatened, retired soon after he penned his withering dissent in appeals court and moved away with his wife, also to New York City. He died there in 1968; Rev. De Laine died six years later.

CHAPTER 16

Student Revolt

IN 1950, BARBARA ROSE JOHNS was fifteen years old and a high school sophomore in Farmville, Virginia. She was born in New York City to parents who had emigrated north in hope of better fortunes. But Harlem during the Depression was an unforgiving place for two people with no job skills, and so, after barely surviving in a series of menial jobs, Robert and Violet Johns returned home to Prince Edward County.

Barbara attended Robert Russa Moton High School, the county's only school for African Americans. Its conditions were nightmarish. The school was horribly overcrowded, with a roof that leaked, no gymnasium or cafeteria, and heated only with potbellied stoves. Students had to sit under umbrellas when it rained and crowd near the stoves in winter. "There was no running water," John Stokes, student body vice president, recounted later, "which meant no matter how hot or cold it was we had to go out to the outdoor toilets, which were terrible, really. There was no flushing. Sometimes you looked down and there were maggots crawling around." Some of the newer classrooms were made of tar paper, and the textbooks, when there were any, were out-of-date and in terrible repair, most with broken bindings and pages missing.

It is sad testament to the education of people of color in the South that Moton High School, rather than being the exception, was not much different from other black high schools across the region. And, here as there, both students and parents were supposed to accept what they were given without complaint. "I came to realize," John Stokes said later, "that by . . . providing schools that were grossly unequal to the ones white children attended, the white power structure was programming us to fail."

But Barbara Johns was unwilling to either accept the crumbs of an education or be programmed to fail. Although she was close with her parents, she was inspired by her uncle. Rev. Vernon Johns was an early pioneer of the civil rights movement, educated at Oberlin Seminary and the University of Chicago, who at one point refused to move to the back of an Alabama bus and instead asked for his money back. At the time his niece Barbara was struggling through decrepit Moton High School, Vernon Johns was pastor at the famed Dexter Avenue Baptist Church in Montgomery, Alabama.

Henrietta Hilton, front left, and her fellow students in their ninth grade classroom in Summerton, South Carolina, June 4, 1954. The original wooden school structure was at the heart of one of the four cases involving "separate but equal" facilities.

When he left the church in May 1953, he was replaced by a highly thought-of young pastor named Martin Luther King Jr. Uncle and niece had always kept in close touch.

Black parents had been complaining to the local school board about the shoddy conditions at Moton for years. Finally, at the beginning of the fall 1950 term, in the wake

of Supreme Court decisions that had begun to threaten segregation as an institution, the board announced that they
had decided to build a new school for African American students. Then nothing. No land was purchased, no plans were
drawn up, no building contractors were hired.

In October 1950, Barbara Johns decided that black
families had waited long enough. She began to talk to local
parents, teachers, the school principal, and fellow students
about taking some positive action. But everyone, even most
of the students, was afraid to confront the white officials
who controlled the county. Every time they were asked, the
school board insisted no action would be necessary, that
the new school would be built.

By spring 1951, there had still been no progress. For
the parents and members of the school faculty, this seemed
to be just one more occasion on which they were helpless to
improve their conditions. But with Barbara Johns and a few
of her classmates leading the way, the students had come to
feel differently.

On April 23, the school principal, Boyd Jones, received
a telephone call. The voice on the other end was difficult
to make out—it seemed like a bad connection—but Jones
finally realized the caller was telling him that two of his
students were in the Greyhound bus terminal and he needed
to get there right away or the police would be called. As
soon as Jones had rushed from the school building, Barbara

Johns and a small group of conspirators sent notes to every classroom, instructing the teachers to bring their students to the auditorium. They signed the notes with the principal's initial.

Soon, 450 students and 24 teachers were stuffed into the small auditorium—the school had been built to hold 180 children—with the threadbare curtain on the stage pulled shut. When it opened, Barbara Johns was standing next to a row of chairs in which her fellow conspirators were seated. She asked the teachers to leave.

She then addressed the student body and told them that they deserved a better school to attend and if no one else would do anything about it, they should do it themselves. And the way to begin was for every student in the school to walk out. And every student did.

The strike lasted two weeks. The whites on the school board were at a loss as to how to respond. They couldn't put 400-plus students in jail, and arresting only Barbara Johns, John Stokes, Carrie Stokes, his sister and the student body president, and the other leaders would most certainly be covered by every major newspaper in America. But spending the money on a new black school was also out of the question. As the walkout continued, parents who had been fearful of the outcome began to rally to the students' cause. The local pastor, L. Francis Griffin, was vocal in his support. Finally, T. J. McIlwaine, the school superintendent,

tried to end the walkout by meeting with the students and telling them that Moton High School was as good as any other black school, and that money would soon be allocated for an even nicer school.

What had worked with the parents, however, did not work with Barbara Johns and Carrie and John Stokes. With Rev. Griffin's help, they contacted the Virginia NAACP, which dispatched lawyers Oliver Hill and Spottswood Robinson to Farmville.

With *Briggs v. Elliott* almost certain to be destined for the Supreme Court, Hill and Robinson pledged NAACP support, but only if the students dropped their demand for a new school and instead insisted on full integration. Barbara Johns thought, "It seemed like reaching for the moon. But we had great faith in Mr. Robinson and Mr. Hill." The two lawyers told the students that their parents would need to support full integration as well.

Although the students were eager to move ahead, parents and the staff of Moton High School realized how big a risk such a lawsuit would represent. Beyond the threat of physical violence, which was very real, anyone employed at the school could lose his or her job, as could any parent who worked for a white employer. Mortgages could be called in, with anyone who could not pay thrown out of their home. Prince Edward County functioned not all that differently than during the slave era, so it would take immense courage for the black community to band together to demand such a radical step.

But they did.

On May 23, 1951, only days before *Briggs v. Elliott* would be decided in appeals court, 117 students of Moton High School filed a lawsuit in federal court to end segregation in public schools. The first name on that list was Dorothy Davis and so the case would be recorded as *Davis v. County School Board of Prince Edward County*. No lower court was going to be willing to take the radical step of overruling *Plessy*, and so this case, like *Briggs v. Elliott*, with which it would be combined, could not be settled anywhere but the Supreme Court building in Washington, DC. By the time that occurred, school boards in two other states and the District of Columbia would be involved, making what would be called *Brown v. Board of Education* a nationwide assault on white supremacy.

CHAPTER 17

Kansas

T HE CASE THAT would become the most famous of those
decided by the Supreme Court on May 17, 1954, might
have seemed the least likely. Topeka, in Shawnee County,
Kansas, bore little resemblance to Clarendon County, South
Carolina, or Prince Edward County, Virginia. Unlike the
Southern counties where African Americans were either in
the majority or close to it, Topeka was less than ten percent
black. Segregation was not required by law in any public
schools and only allowed in elementary schools in cities
with populations of more than fifteen thousand. Facilities at
black schools were equal to those in white schools or close to
it, and many teachers were excellent, sometimes superior
to those at white schools, and well paid. If a black child was
forced to attend an elementary school farther away from his
or her home than a white school, bus service was provided;
there was no bus service for white schools.

In addition, Kansas law forbade discrimination in hotels and restaurants, and bus or train transportation and waiting rooms were integrated. In many ways, unlike in South Carolina and Virginia, where segregation was at the hub of the daily lives of both races, in Kansas it seemed to have been casually stuck on.

But Topeka, Kansas, had its own version of Jim Crow and was equally determined to maintain it. Only one hotel in the city would accept black guests, no matter what the law said, and whites rarely stayed there. Few restaurants would serve black diners. Five of the seven of Topeka's movie theaters would not sell tickets to African Americans, one would sell them only balcony seats, and one theater was for people of color only. The city swimming pool was whites only, except one day a year when people of color could swim there as well.

The most pronounced segregation was in the supposedly integrated high school. Although both races attended the same classes, there were separate music programs, sports programs, and even two student councils. The white and black basketball teams had different nicknames. African American students attended "good-nigger assemblies," while white students were in chapel. There were white and black school "kings and queens."

Twelve Kansas cities met the population cutoff for elementary school segregation and ten of those, including Topeka, had opted for full segregation. In Topeka, eighteen elementary schools were white, and four were African American. For most of the first half of the twentieth century, Topeka's black population seemed to accept this arrangement, especially since high-quality teachers allowed their children to receive a good early education. However, "following World War II, a new generation of black leaders appeared in Topeka. Many were veterans and had performed military service of the same kind and quality as white participants in the war. Hence, they were unwilling to accept a diluted kind of citizenship in their own community."

Oliver Brown, who worked for the railroad and was a part-time minister, was one of those who refused to have his citizenship diluted. As the summer of 1950 was drawing to a close, Brown's eight-year-old daughter, Linda, was preparing to be enrolled in third grade. She lived in a racially mixed neighborhood and had a number of white playmates. Instead of the Charles Sumner School, named for the ferociously abolitionist Massachusetts senator, and closest to her home, she was assigned to an all-black school twenty-two blocks away. Not only would she not attend school with her playmates, Linda would have to struggle simply to get to the black school. As her father later testified, "In order for Linda to catch the bus at the pick up point it was necessary for her to leave home at 7:40 a.m., walk six blocks, passing through a railroad switchyard and crossing Kansas Avenue at a time when motor traffic was heaviest; the school bus was

The Brown family: Linda Brown (left), her parents, Leola and Oliver, and little sister, Terry Lynn, stand in front of their house, Topeka, Kansas, 1954.

Linda Brown.

often late and on those occasions Linda often waited for long periods on the unsheltered street, exposed to cold, rain, and snow; and on other occasions she arrived at school before the doors were unlocked and was forced to wait outside the building."

On the first day of school, Oliver Brown brought his daughter to Sumner to register but both were turned away.

Oliver Brown had decided that his daughter should be able to attend school without regard to the color of her skin. A boyhood friend, Charles Scott, a lawyer in practice with his father, Elisha, who was a local courtroom legend, agreed and suggested Brown do something about it.

Elisha J. Scott was a native of Topeka, born in 1890, and was one of the first African Americans to graduate from Washburn University Law School, an integrated college in the city's downtown that had been founded by abolitionists. Almost immediately, Scott gained notoriety for taking on cases for black or poor white clients who either could not find another lawyer or couldn't pay for one. While Scott was competent in his knowledge of the law, he was near brilliant at trial. A small man, always in a suit that was too big for him, and prone to take a drink or two or three, Scott was a shameless showman with a devastating wit. In argument, he could evoke from judges, jurors, and even opposing counsel tears or laughter, sometimes both in the course of the same speech. Scott racked up an incredible record, winning any number of cases where victory had seemed impossible, including in segregation and equal rights. He was totally dedicated to those he represented, and eventually two of his sons, John and Charles, had joined his law firm.

Precisely at the moment Oliver Brown was refused at Sumner School, Charles Scott, in conjunction with the local NAACP branch, was seeking out parents who would join in an action against the local school board.

But the Scotts were not the only crusaders willing to take on Topeka Jim Crow. Esther Brown, no relation to Linda and Oliver, would also unflinchingly pursue equal rights in Kansas, even though terrorists threatened to burn down her house or murder her, the FBI opened a file on her after she was accused of being a communist—they concluded she "actively agitated Negroes, getting them to assert their right to send children to school for white children"—the police harassed her, and her husband was fired from his job by his own father.

If Elisha and Charles Scott were unlikely lawyers, Esther Brown was perhaps a more unlikely activist. She was white, Jewish, and, before 1947, when she was thirty years old, had been a typical suburban housewife. Raised in Kansas City, she had married an army air corps World War II veteran who worked in his father's business, had two daughters, and moved into a nice home on a clean, quiet street in Merriam, just outside the city in which she had been raised. The only black person she knew well enough to speak with was her maid.

Elisha J. Scott.

But one day, that maid, Helen Swann, told her employer of a bond issue to build a sparkling new elementary school for white children. Black children would continue to attend the two-room Walker School in neighboring South Park. It was nearly one hundred years old, had no indoor plumbing or heat, no bathrooms, no cafeteria, a dirt playground, no principal, only two teachers, and no new textbooks. In addition to being forced to use a filthy outhouse, all students, including first graders, would need to walk home if they wanted to eat lunch. To get home, Helen Swann's daughters would pass directly in front of the new white school.

All this was against Kansas law, because Merriam's population was less than fifteen thousand, but no one seemed to care.

Esther Brown thought this appalling, told people so, met privately with school board members, and attended the next public school board meeting. To open the meeting, the head of the school board addressed the 350 people present. "All of a sudden we seem to have a racial problem in South Park. Well, let me tell you that no nigger will get in South Park as long as I live."

Then Esther Brown stood. "I'm just a Kansas housewife," she replied. "I don't represent these people, but I've seen the conditions of their school. I know none of you would want your children educated under such circumstances. They're not asking for integration, just a fair shake."

Esther Brown.

The assembled parents screamed jeers and insults at her, and one woman struck her with an umbrella. The school board, likely just to mock her, voted to install new light bulbs in the black school.

Soon afterward, she received threatening telephone calls. Many people in her neighborhood refused to speak to her. Others insulted her on the street. They might have felt safe in doing so, because Esther Brown had been respectful, even meek, at the meeting.

It would be a fatal miscalculation.

Esther Brown had left the meeting feeling "nauseated," and from there devoted herself totally and fearlessly to gaining equal rights for the black parents and an end to school segregation in her town. She held meetings, organized a local NAACP chapter, asked the Kansas City NAACP to file suit, and then raised money to fund it by asking everyone she knew. She even solicited funds at a Billie Holiday concert, taking thirty black children with her to see the famed African American jazz singer, to help make the point.

The threats against Esther Brown's life and home increased. A cross was burned in her front yard. Some local whites complained to the FBI, and they began an investigation. Her father-in-law fired his son for being married to a communist. She had a miscarriage. But still she kept on.

The Kansas City NAACP finally agreed to file the suit,

but the lawyer they chose did not seem sufficiently committed for Esther Brown. So she hired Elisha J. Scott.

To pay Scott, she raised money wherever she could and borrowed when she could not. She persuaded the black parents to boycott the Walker School and helped them set up a private school to fill the gap. She convinced a community leader, Alfonso Webb, to lend his name to the lawsuit, with his son as the lead plaintiff.

It took almost two years, but in June 1949, the Kansas Supreme Court found in *Webb v. School District No. 90* that the school board had unlawfully segregated the elementary schools and that boys and girls of color should attend the new and generously funded South Park Common Grade School. Segregation in Merriam schools was dead.

Esther Brown and Elisha Scott decided not to stop there but to take their crusade to Scott's hometown of Topeka.

Both the local and national offices of the NAACP had been attempting to negotiate with the Topeka school board, trying to find a means to end segregation that could be supported by at least much of the community. They had gotten nowhere. But the NAACP could not mount a challenge in court unless some of those wronged by segregation—students of color and their parents—were willing to have the action initiated in their names. At the time, Charles Scott was one of those working with the NAACP to recruit black parents willing to take the risk of suing a white school board. Esther Brown, fresh from the victory in Merriam, helped convince the African American parents that they could win in Topeka as well.

Oliver Brown quickly agreed to join with twelve other parents, representing their twenty children, in filing suit against the Topeka school board in United States district court. Their claim was that the segregated schools to which they were forced to send their children were inferior to white schools and also, attacking *Plessy* head-on, that racial segregation in public education was by definition a denial of equal protection of the laws.

As always, the NAACP expected to lose in the lower courts, and it did. But this time, there was an unexpected wrinkle. The three judges wrote in their decision, "Segregation of white and colored children in public schools has a detrimental effect upon the colored children. The impact is greater when it has the sanction of the law; for the policy of separating the races is usually interpreted as denoting the inferiority of the Negro group. A sense of inferiority affects the motivation of a child to learn. Segregation with the sanction of law, therefore, has a tendency to retard the educational and mental development of Negro children and to deprive them of some of the benefits they would receive in a racially integrated school system."

Although the appeals court did not feel it had the

standing to overrule *Plessy*, these were exactly the arguments the NAACP had been making in public but had been hesitant to put forth in a courtroom. Now, however, the arguments were on the record for everyone, including the nine justices of the Supreme Court, to see.

CHAPTER 18

The Battle Is Joined

FRED VINSON IS probably the only person ever to be appointed to the Supreme Court because of a seat at a poker table.

When Chief Justice Harlan Fiske Stone died in April 1946, he left a Court in disarray. So deep were the divisions that two of the justices, Robert Jackson and Hugo Black, were publicly feuding about their views on the law, an unheard-of breach of Court etiquette. Jackson wanted very much to be chief justice, and when President Truman did not appoint him, he accused Black of sabotaging his chances, even sending notes to Congress defending his positions.

But Hugo Black was not the cause of Jackson's being passed over. Harry Truman was clever enough to know that he could not have a member of either faction in the chief justice's chair. That would be a declaration of who had won the battle and who had lost, and the bitterness would simply deepen. Instead, he needed someone who could end the conflict, a man who could at least persuade the justices to restrict their bickering to questions of legal theory. For this he chose his friend and poker buddy, Fred Vinson, a heavy-jowled, sad-eyed baseball fanatic.

Vinson was raised in a small town in Kentucky, where his father was the local jailer, and had worked his way up from local office to state office to winning a congressional seat at the height of the Great Depression in 1933. In his twenty years in Washington, Vinson had done almost everything in government, serving in all three branches. He went from Congress to being a federal judge, gave up his lifetime appointment to head a price control office for President Roosevelt during the Second World War, became friends with President Truman after Roosevelt's death, was appointed Truman's secretary of the treasury, and quickly became the most influential member of the president's cabinet. Finally, in 1946, Frederick Moore Vinson became a nominee for chief justice of the Supreme Court of the United States and was confirmed without objection by the Senate.

Although Vinson was unable to totally quell the animosity among his fellow justices, he was such a thoroughly decent man that the public feuding largely ended. On the bench, he proved more loyal to Harry S. Truman's initiatives in equal rights than to his segregationist Kentucky origins.

He presided over *Shelley v. Kraemer*, *Sweatt v. Painter*, and *McLaurin v. Oklahoma Regents*, and succeeded in securing unanimous votes in each case. But overturning *Plessy v. Ferguson* was another matter entirely. Four of the nine justices were from the South, and others, especially Jackson and Felix Frankfurter, were deeply rooted in upholding precedent unless an extraordinary reason could be fashioned for ignoring it. Gaining a unanimous or near unanimous decision—which seemed a requirement if the verdict was to be accepted in the South—was going to be difficult if not impossible.

Vinson likely would have preferred avoiding taking the issue on at all, but that was no longer an option. And so, in June 1952, the Court agreed to hear *Brown v. Board of Education* and *Briggs v. Elliott* in the coming term, which would begin in October. But three other segregation cases were also heading for the Supreme Court. *Davis v. County School Board of Prince Edward County* had been decided in district court that March, and there were additional actions against school boards in Delaware and the District of Columbia.

When the fall term commenced, only days before Thurgood Marshall and Robert Carter were due to appear before the high bench, Chief Justice Vinson announced a postponement. Their two cases would be heard in December, with three other cases folded in: *Davis v. Prince Edward*

The Supreme Court justices who first heard the segregation cases, presided over by Frederick Moore Vinson.

County; the District of Columbia case, *Bolling v. Sharpe*; and the Delaware case, *Gebhart v. Belton*. Hearing all five cases together was an announcement that segregation was not restricted to the South but was instead a national issue.

The most important equal rights trial in Supreme Court history began at 1:35 p.m. on Tuesday, December 9, 1952. The cases would be heard one at a time, beginning with *Brown v. Board of Education of Topeka*, and would take until Thursday to complete. From there, it was expected to be months before the Supreme Court rendered its verdict.

Portrait of the African American students for whom the famous Brown v. Board of Education *case was brought, and their parents: (front row left to right) Vicki Henderson, Donald Henderson, Linda Brown, James Emanuel, Nancy Todd, and Katherine Carper; (back row left to right) Zelma Henderson, Oliver Brown, Sadie Emanuel, Lucinda Todd, and Lena Carper; Topeka, Kansas, 1953.*

For the event, the *New York Times* reported, "The Supreme Court chamber was filled to its capacity of about 300 when the arguments began. It appeared that nearly half of those were Negroes." Another 450 waited in the corridors, hoping to get in. What the paper did not mention was that for a trial on segregation, the seats in the Supreme Court gallery had been given out with no preference for race, and the seating was fully integrated.

As the hearing began, Robert Carter, described in the newspapers as "a Negro lawyer," speaking for the Topeka parents, went immediately to the issue. "We abandon any claim of constitutional inequality except what comes from segregation itself, which denies Negro children equal protection of the law. The only concern of the Constitution is educational inequality, independent of physical facilities." There would be no hiding, either by the lawyers or the justices. The only question was whether the very act of separation created inequality, in violation of Fourteenth Amendment guarantees.

When Justice Frankfurter asked Carter whether he was asking that *Plessy* be overturned even though more than a dozen states had relied on that decision to set up their educational facilities, Carter confirmed that was precisely what he was asking. That left the lawyers for the parents to prove that separate could not be equal. But Carter's attempt to do so turned out to be shaky. Rather than discuss the psychological harm to black children forced to attend segregated schools, he focused his argument on a claim that *Sweatt* and *McLaurin* had overruled *Plessy*. In those cases, Carter insisted, the plaintiffs had demonstrated that black students could not get the same quality education as was available in white schools. Most legal scholars believed that beyond graduate education, *Sweatt* and *McLaurin* had done no such thing. The attorney for Kansas, who had never been to Washington and had been assigned the case only weeks before, simply stated that a state had the right to send children to

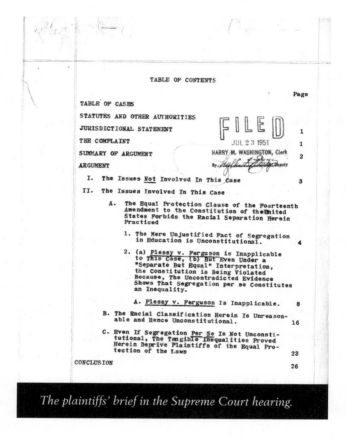

TABLE OF CONTENTS

Page

FILED

JUL 23 1951

HARRY M. WASHINGTON, Clerk

By _____ Deputy

The plaintiffs' brief in the Supreme Court hearing.

schools as they saw fit, as was guaranteed in *Plessy*, which was still, at the least for the moment, the law of the land.

When Brown was concluded, *Briggs v. Elliott* was next, and so it was Thurgood Marshall's turn.

If Robert Carter had faced an inexperienced and unknown foe, Marshall's opposing counsel could not have been more different. The attorney for South Carolina was

John W. Davis, considered perhaps the finest appeals lawyer in the nation. He had also been a member of Congress, solicitor general, ambassador to Great Britain, and, in 1924, the Democratic nominee for president of the United States. All nine justices, each of whom he knew personally, held Davis in the highest esteem.

Against the titan, Marshall would get a short reprieve. Little could be accomplished in the time remaining on December 9, so the arguments were held over until the following day. The gallery was again full, once more with at least half the seats filled by African Americans intermixed with whites.

Davis told the Court they had no business meddling in state policy, the perfect out for any justice who wanted to avoid taking an actual position on the race question. "The segregation of pupils in the public schools on the basis of color is not a question of constitutional rights, but of legislative policy." As such, "the court should not set aside as unconstitutional the segregation statutes enacted by the states."

What was more, Davis went on, segregation was a virtue of the American system. "What is the great national policy underlying this whole question? Is it not the fact that the very strength and fiber of our Federal system is local self-government for those matters which local action is competent?" Finally, Davis insisted, segregation was a wise policy because forcing the races together would certainly result in resentment, threats to the rule of law, and even violence.

Marshall, arguing for the Clarendon County parents, insisted that the Constitution was "the supreme law of the land," and so segregation could not be simply state policy since it violated a basic constitutional right of black Americans. He turned the tables on Davis by accusing him of not having enough faith in the very white people he was representing, telling the justices that the South Carolinians were patriotic and law-abiding and that if segregation were against the law, they would accept it. It is likely that every person in the room knew that South Carolina whites would do no such thing, but it left Davis in the position of stating that his clients would not obey the law if they lost.

Marshall was most effective in pointing out to the justices that the evidence that segregation as an institution was damaging to African Americans, be they graduate students or children in third grade, had been acknowledged by both the Supreme Court in *Sweatt* and *McLaurin* and the lower courts in both *Brown* and this very case. South Carolina, he told the justices, had made no effort to deny or refute this basic truth. In fact, they didn't seem to care. And so, inflicting damage on a group of citizens simply because their skin color was different was as clear a denial of equal protection of the law as it was possible to make.

Virginia was up next, and one of the justices, Robert Jackson, who had prosecuted Nazi war criminals at the end of World War II, asked Spottswood Robinson, representing the Virginia students, whether Congress should pass a law declaring segregation contrary to public policy. This seemed to be a trap, questioning whether ending segregation was a matter for the legislature and not the courts, as John Davis had declared. If Robinson replied that he would welcome an act of Congress, it would help give cover to the justices who did not wish to be forced to decide on the question. But he did not. He said Congress could pass such legislation, but it would not matter because the Constitution had already spoken on the issue. Virginia's lawyer agreed that Congress was not the place to decide on segregation, that a new and separate constitutional amendment was required, an impossibility since three-quarters of the states would never agree.

James Nabrit, another African American, argued *Bolling v. Sharpe*, which was different from the other four cases because the District of Columbia is federal, not state, territory, so equal protection fell under the Fifth Amendment rather than the Fourteenth. Nabrit, who would later become president of Howard University and represent the United States at the United Nations, was perhaps the best orator of any of the attorneys in the five cases. He made the point that segregation in Washington had not been mandatory by law but had merely been imposed as a convenience to whites.

The lawyers for the NAACP Legal Defense team: (from left) Louis L. Redding, Robert L. Carter, Oliver W. Hill, Thurgood Marshall, Spottswood W. Robinson III, Jack Greenberg, James S. Nabrit, and George E. C. Hayes.

"We submit that in this case, in the heart of the nation's capital, in the capital of democracy, in the capital of the free world, there is no place for a segregated school system. This country cannot afford it, and the Constitution does not permit it, and statutes of Congress do not authorize it."

The black children's cause was helped immensely when the attorney for the school board, trying to make the point that the Constitution could not be broadened to suit expansions of social policy, quoted from *Dred Scott v. Sandford*, the most notorious decision in American history. In his opinion, Chief Justice Roger B. Taney had written that "people who were imported as slaves [or] their descendents" were "beings of an inferior order and altogether unfit to associate with the white race, either in social or political relations; and so far inferior that they had no rights which the white man was bound to respect."

The Delaware case was unlike the other four. State courts had ruled for the parents and ordered the state board of education to integrate its schools, but the board had refused until a ruling came from the United States Supreme Court. Delaware's position was much the same as the other defendants'—the state intended to equalize the schools and so the *Plessy* mandate would be satisfied. Arguing for the parents, Louis Redding and Jack Greenberg—the only white lawyer to appear for the plaintiffs—simply repeated the point that segregation meant inequality and no amount of money spent to improve black schools would change that.

From there, the justices retired to try to find a way to legally, politically, and morally deal with a system that was the direct descendant of slavery. The outcome was hardly assured. As he was leaving the courtroom, John Davis of South Carolina was overheard to say he was certain they had won, that segregation would be upheld, at least by 5–4, but maybe even 6–3.

CHAPTER 19

A Change at the Top

B UT JOHN DAVIS, Thurgood Marshall, and the other
African American lawyers, and the entire nation would
have to wait. The months dragged on without a decision. The
wounds that Fred Vinson had been appointed to heal still
festered, perhaps even grew worse. The only change was that
the rivalries were no longer on public view. Almost everyone
agreed that the Court needed to speak with one voice about
segregation, but less than one case in five brought before
these nine justices was decided unanimously, an extremely
low number. While Vinson was a skilled politician, he was
not a strong leader, and achieving consensus seemed impossible. To make the situation worse, no one seemed to know
how Vinson himself would vote on the question.

Finally, as the term was nearing its end in June 1953,
with no resolution in sight, Justice Frankfurter suggested an

unusual strategy—find a way to hold the decision over until the fall term. That was no guarantee, of course, that matters would improve just by waiting four months, but at least the Court would not be forced to admit that they couldn't resolve the most important case to come before them. But the justices needed an excuse, so they devised a series of very technical questions. Some were on the origins and intent of the Fourteenth Amendment, and others were on how integration would be implemented if the Court struck down *Plessy*. Contrivance or not, preparing answers would require the lawyers to work nonstop all summer and then appear for the rehearing, set for October 12.

Then, on September 8, 1953, Fred Vinson had a heart attack and died.

There was a new president, Dwight D. Eisenhower, a Republican, the first of his party to occupy the White House in twenty years. Eisenhower had secured the nomination in a closely divided convention only with the help of California governor Earl Warren. Eisenhower himself said, "If anyone ever clinched the nomination for me, it was Earl Warren." Warren had been mentioned as a potential nominee for vice president, but when Eisenhower chose California congressman Richard Nixon instead, he told Warren that, if elected, he would nominate Warren for the first Supreme Court seat that opened up. Which he did.

Although he would
not be officially confirmed
until the following March,
Earl Warren took his seat
as chief justice in October
1953. The *Brown* rehear-
ing was then rescheduled
for December.

On first blush, Warren's
appointment would have
seemed to doom the inte-
gration cases. While not
having much of a record

Earl Warren.

in dealing with African Americans, Warren had a notorious background of racism against Asian Americans. He
had been a member of the Native Sons of the Golden West,
which, at the time he joined, viewed America as a white
people's nation and later favored confiscation of property
from Japanese Americans and even their expulsion from the
United States. At one point, as California's attorney general,
Warren endorsed a lawsuit that would have denied birth-
right citizenship to children of Japanese immigrants because
"the Declaration of Independence and the Constitution were
created by and for white people."

But it was in his response to the Japanese attack on Pearl
Harbor, again during Warren's tenure as attorney general,

when whites' long-simmering distaste for Japanese Americans boiled over, that the full extent of his racism was revealed.

In the wake of the attack, many California whites were convinced that Japanese Americans had a greater loyalty to Japan than to the United States, and that many were spies and traitors bent on sabotage and preparing the West Coast for invasion. Military and civilian authorities wanted to know where Japanese Americans lived and owned land that could be used as staging areas for anti-American activity. Under Attorney General Warren's direction, an official in each county was assigned to locate and map all Japanese-occupied land. When the survey was complete, Warren forwarded the results to the army. He "executed this mission with the precision of a military operation, using large scale maps of each reporting county drawn to uniform scale. He instructed his subordinates that, 'All property which is owned, controlled or occupied by persons of the Japanese race, whether citizens or not, should be marked on the maps in red.' He also asked each county official to designate 'important installations' so that proximity of Japanese Californians could be easily compared."

When the maps had been drawn, Warren concluded, "The Japanese situation as it exists in California today may well be the Achilles heel of the entire civilian defense effort. Unless something is done, it may bring about a repetition of Pearl Harbor." And something to be done that Earl Warren

Japanese Americans at an internment camp following the attack on Pearl Harbor.

supported was the removal of more than 100,000 American citizens of Japanese ancestry from their homes, and their deportation to what were in all but name concentration camps away from the Pacific Coast. This would be the only time in United States history when American citizens were interned by force, and without trial, based only on their race.

To ensure that Congress and President Franklin Roosevelt

would support such an extreme measure, Warren testified before the House of Representatives Select Committee Investigating National Defense Migration, which had traveled to San Francisco for the hearings. He told the committee that he was convinced that the "distribution of the Japanese population appears to manifest something more than coincidence." Japanese Americans, he added, were "ideally situated with reference to points of strategic importance, to carry into execution a tremendous program of sabotage on a mass scale should any considerable number of them be inclined to do so." The congressmen were suitably impressed, although it turned out that Warren's definition of *strategic installation* had been contrived to suit his conclusions and that there were other serious flaws in his methods. There was, in fact, no threat at all, and Japanese Americans would turn out to be more intensely patriotic than white America deserved.

But none of that mattered. American citizens whose only crime was not looking white were shunted off to spend the war behind barbed wire, denied the very sort of constitutionally guaranteed equal rights that black people were trying to shame nine white men into granting them. To make matters worse, Warren was a man known for the unwillingness to admit an error or a mistake, and nothing in the public record gave Thurgood Marshall or the other attorneys prosecuting the *Brown* cases reason to think anything had changed.

Yet it had.

For reasons Earl Warren never made clear, the enormity of what he had done had overwhelmed him. He wrote later that he "deeply regretted the removal order and my own testimony advocating it, because it was not in keeping with our American concept of freedom and the rights of citizens . . . Whenever I thought of the innocent little children who were torn from home, school friends, and congenial surroundings, I was conscience-stricken . . . It was wrong to react so impulsively, without positive evidence of disloyalty."

So instead of a man with an unabashed, unapologetic history of discrimination ascending to the chief justice's chair, Thurgood Marshall and his fellows got a guilt-ridden penitent, anxious to atone for past misdeeds.

CHAPTER 20

Round Two

O N DECEMBER 8, 1953, just one day short of the anniversary of the first trial, eight of the nine justices who had been unable to decide whether segregation was an evil in violation of the Constitution or simply another way of looking at race relations, sat down to try again. The ninth justice, the new chief, would be responsible for achieving what his predecessor, a master politician, had not—agreement among the others, who had been at war for years.

As before, this second trial would take three days, although the order of the cases had changed. During the course of the hearings, the chief justice did not say very much, leaving the bulk of the questioning to the eight men who had sat in before. Although this hearing was supposed to focus on the dense technical material the Court had asked the lawyers to prepare over the summer, it was in fact largely a rehearing of the same material from a year before. The

Harold Boulware, Thurgood Marshall, and Spottswood Robinson before the rehearing.

lawyers were the same, as was the gist of the questions to which they were asked to respond.

When it was all done, the nine justices retired to consider the same simple question: Did segregation in and of itself violate the equal protection guarantees written into the Constitution to ensure that all people were treated equally? In spite of what Henry Billings Brown had written in *Plessy v. Ferguson*, could people be equal if they were forced to be separate? Neither the justices nor anyone else were under any illusions—although these cases focused only on schools, if *Plessy* fell here, it would soon fall everywhere else, and the social structure under which the South had functioned for more than a half century would be ripped apart. *Brown v. Board of Education* had been widely referred to as "the trial of the century," but it would be more appropriate to call it "the trial of America."

No one expected a quick decision.

During the next months, the justices would deliberate in darkness. There were no news reports, leaks, or even hints as to what was going on. Only afterward, in the days, weeks, and even years after the reporters ran upstairs to hear Chief Justice Warren read the opinion of the Court from his seat at the center of the long bench behind which the justices sat, did some of what transpired begin to sift out.

The New York Yankee Hall of Fame pitcher Lefty Gomez once said, "It's better to be lucky than good." Earl Warren was both. He turned out to be a good deal more skillful in managing the warring justices' egos than Vinson had been. He consulted with both Hugo Black and Robert Jackson without taking sides; asked questions on legal theory of Felix Frankfurter, the Court's premier scholar; showed great sympathy for Tom Clark and Stanley Reed, two Southerners

whose votes would be necessary if *Plessy* was to be suc-cessfully overturned; and was accessible and open on all questions of procedure and personality.

But he was lucky as well. The year off had softened much of the hostility between the factions and also made even clearer that with African Americans more and more a factor in mainstream American life, maintaining what was simply a watered-down version of slavery was no lon-ger realistic. Warren himself, other than his terrible lack of judgment about Japanese Americans, was an essentially decent man—if he were not, he would not have been guilt-ridden—and he transmitted that spirit to his fellow justices. Although their verdict would need to be couched in law, Warren succeeded in having even the most rigorously legal-istic justices—Jackson and Frankfurter—see the issue in human terms as well.

Still, with personalities, intellects, and views on the law so different, any decision that all nine men could endorse was going to have to weave its way through a number of vari-ables. What would be acceptable to William O. Douglas, the Court's most liberal justice, was unlikely to be acceptable to Robert Jackson. Justices in the center feared rendering a decision that would result in the South's ignoring the Court's instruction, possibly by violent means. Then there were the Southerners.

With Fred Vinson's death, the four Southerners on

the bench had been reduced to three. Hugo Black, from Alabama, a member of the Ku Klux Klan in his youth, had become one of the most progressive justices, and his vote to end segregation had never been in doubt. But Tom Clark, from Texas, considered a no vote in 1952—he would have demanded equalization—seemed willing to go along a year later. His only condition was that integration not be done like an ax falling on the neck of Southern society, but initiated in a manner to cause the least disruption. Only Stanley Reed from Kentucky could not see a path to a ruling, although he, too, had become forced to admit that segregation had been used to repress and subjugate people of color.

Warren negotiated his way through this hall of mirrors brilliantly, incorporating suggestions from all sides in a way that might be distasteful but not deal-breaking to others. He had the advantage of everyone on the Court realizing that *Brown v. Board of Education* was not simply a legal matter but a political question that might very well define the United States of America for future generations.

Still, the going was slow. Then, Justice Jackson suffered a heart attack and was hospitalized. His demands did not go away, but he lessened them to a point that Warren could accede without fear of others' defection. Felix Frankfurter had decided to be a yes vote as well. Almost as important as their willingness to rule for the plaintiffs was their agreement not to write separate opinions, which could easily have

Earl Warren's Supreme Court, which ultimately decided on the groundbreaking segregation cases. (Front row, from left to right:) Felix Frankfurter, Hugo Black, Chief Justice Earl Warren, Stanley Reed, and William O. Douglas. Back row, from left to right: Tom Clark, Robert H. Jackson, Harold H. Burton, and Sherman Minton.

raised issues that segregationists could jump on to avoid following the Court's instructions. Warren intended there to be one opinion and that it be clearly stated in terms that ordinary Americans, both black and white, could understand.

In early May 1954, Earl Warren spoke with Stanley Reed, the final holdout. He did not demand, he did not disparage, he did not even try to persuade. He merely told Justice Reed what Reed already knew—anything less than a unanimous opinion could tear the nation apart. Reed finally agreed.

Everything was finally in place. A unanimous court would speak through the chief justice with one voice and, in doing so, change the course of American history. With no further reason for delay, Warren decided on the next available Monday, May 17, 1954, to render the verdict. He made certain that no one, not the other justices, not law clerks, not even the printer, would leak a word of when and with what result *Brown v. Board of Education* would be shared with the nation.

CHAPTER 21

The Meaning of Equality

S HORTLY BEFORE 1:00 p.m., after the reporters had taken seats in the courtroom, Chief Justice Earl Warren began to read the Court's decision. (The opinion in the Washington, DC, case, *Bolling v. Sharpe*, was delivered separately from the other four cases but came to the same conclusion.) Like all opinions read from the bench, the verdict was recited slowly and clearly, without emotion or embellishment:

> These cases come to us from the States of Kansas, South Carolina, Virginia, and Delaware. They are premised on different facts and different local conditions, but a common legal question justifies their consideration together in this consolidated opinion.

Warren's wording was precisely as he had wanted—short, powerful, to the point, and easily understandable by ordinary Americans. But for more than half of his reading, those listening could not be certain for whom the Court would rule.

The chief justice first spoke of what the decision was *not* based on. It would not be based on all the work the lawyers had done over the summer researching the origin and intent of the Fourteenth Amendment. Those questions had been a smokescreen and were now dismissed as such. Warren intoned:

> Re-argument was largely devoted to the circumstances surrounding the adoption of the Fourteenth Amendment in 1868. It covered exhaustively consideration of the Amendment in Congress, ratification by the states, then-existing practices in racial segregation, and the views of proponents and opponents of the Amendment. This discussion and our own investigation convince us that, although these sources cast some light, it is not enough to resolve the problem with which we are faced.

The decision would also not be based on established precedent. *Plessy v. Ferguson* would not determine the Court's ruling:

In approaching this problem, we cannot turn the clock back to 1868, when the Amendment was adopted, or even to 1896, when Plessy v. Ferguson was written. We must consider public education in the light of its full development and its present place in American life throughout the Nation. Only in this way can it be determined if segregation in public schools deprives these plaintiffs of the equal protection of the laws.

Next, Warren talked of the role and importance of public education in American life:

Education is perhaps the most important function of state and local governments. Compulsory school attendance laws and the great expenditures for education both demonstrate our recognition of the importance of education to our democratic society. It is required in the performance of our most basic public responsibilities, even service in the armed forces. It is the very foundation of good citizenship. Today it is a principal instrument in awakening the child to cultural values, in preparing him for later professional training, and in helping him to adjust normally to his environment. In these days, it is doubtful that any child may reasonably be expected to succeed in life if he is denied the opportunity of an education. Such an opportunity, where the state has undertaken to provide it, is a right which must be made available to all on equal terms.

Then, more than two-thirds through the opinion, he got to the main point:

> We come then to the question presented: does segregation of children in public schools solely on the basis of race, even though the physical facilities and other "tangible" factors may be equal, deprive the children of the minority group of equal educational opportunities? We believe that it does.

There it was. Separate could not be equal. *Plessy v. Ferguson* would be thrown aside, at least in public education. But Earl Warren was not done. The reason behind that conclusion would shock legal scholars. To many, it was not even really "law" at all. The chief justice continued:

> To separate them from others of similar age and qualifications solely because of their race generates a feeling of inferiority as to their status in the community that may affect their hearts and minds in a way unlikely ever to be undone.

To support this conclusion, the opinion contained a footnote citing the work not of law professors but rather of psychologists and social scientists, the first of whom was Kenneth Clark, who had based his conclusions on his highly disputed "doll tests." *New York Times* columnist James Reston, in an article he titled "A Sociological Decision," wrote that the Court relied "more on social scientists than legal precedent" and accepted instead a "test of contemporary social justice."

That the Supreme Court based its decision not on bloodless questions of textbook law but on real-world circumstances proved to be immensely controversial, yet most Americans agreed and more would come to agree that the justices had done their most important job—to right a terrible wrong. As Warren wrote:

> We conclude that, in the field of public education, the doctrine of "separate but equal" has no place. Separate educational facilities are inherently unequal. Therefore, we hold that the plaintiffs and others similarly situated for whom the actions have been brought are, by reason of the segregation complained of, deprived of the equal protection of the laws guaranteed by the Fourteenth Amendment.

NAACP lawyers George Hayes, Thurgood Marshall, and James Nabrit celebrating their victory.

Still, although the Court had declared that, at least in public education, Jim Crow was dead, it was not yet to be gone. In order to gain a unanimous decision, Warren had promised Justices Clark and Reed that the South would not simply be thrown into chaos, and so the chief justice ordered a second hearing in which segregationists would explain just how—and when—they intended to comply with the ruling.

That would prove to be a thorny issue indeed.

CHAPTER 22

Making It Real

R EACTION TO THE decision was immediate but in some cases surprising. While most Southern whites did little to hide their fury—Georgia governor Herman Talmadge said "there will never be mixed schools while I am governor," and school integration could lead to "bloodshed"—others were willing to wait and see just how serious a threat they were actually facing. John F. Byrnes, governor of South Carolina and a former Supreme Court justice, was "shocked" at the decision but urged "all of our people, white and colored, to exercise restraint and preserve order." As Byrnes also pointed out, the Court had not imposed a deadline by which integration had to be achieved, or provided any mechanism to ensure that it actually happened. Those questions would be the subject of the second hearing, scheduled for October.

But for the NAACP, while they were aware there were

battles yet to be fought, this was the victory they had fought so hard to achieve. That school segregation had been struck down on Fourteenth Amendment "equal protection" grounds meant that other areas of segregation should be seen also as "unequal." Within hours of the verdict being read in Washington, Walter White promised, "We will use the courts, legislation, and public opinion to crack the iron curtain in segregation in housing." Discrimination in hiring would be next. Thurgood Marshall, who thirteen years later would be the first African American to sit on the very court that had issued this historic ruling, predicted that school segregation would be eliminated within five years. By 1963, he told reporters, the one hundredth anniversary of the Emancipation Proclamation, segregation in all forms will have disappeared. Waties Waring, by then living in New York, praised the ruling, hoping it would "erase the shame" of previous court decisions that had denied equality to people of color for more than half a century.

African American newspapers were jubilant. The *Chicago Defender* wrote, "Neither the atom bomb nor the hydrogen bomb will ever be as meaningful to our democracy as the unanimous verdict of the Supreme Court that racial segregation violates the spirit and the letter of our Constitution. This means the beginning of the end of the dual society in American life and the system of segregation that supports it."

But White, Marshall, and black newspapers were premature. Before even twenty-four hours had passed, whites were openly discussing ways to avoid integration, everything from simply ignoring the Court to closing down the public school system entirely and giving white families tax breaks to send their children to "private academies." Segregation was not going to be eliminated without a fight.

The fight would not begin in earnest until April 1955, when the Court heard arguments about how—and when—integration would be achieved. The original October 1954 date had been pushed back because Southern states claimed to need time to formulate plans to implement a change so massive. Chief Justice Warren granted the delay, hoping the extra time would allow the Southern states to come to greater acceptance of the Court's decision. In addition, Justice Jackson had died from a second heart attack and was replaced by John Marshall Harlan, the grandson of the one man who had stood against *Plessy* and declared "the Constitution is color blind."

But when the case was reheard, it quickly became clear that forging the right path would be every bit as difficult as deciding whether segregation could continue—perhaps more so.

The first question was "How soon?" Should the Court demand full integration immediately, so that children such as Linda Brown and Barbara Johns need not continue to suffer inferior conditions, or allow integration to proceed gradually, so that school districts could work through the massive logistical problems?

Then there was "How?" Most African American children, precisely because of segregation, were economically worse off than their white counterparts and were not learning at the same grade level. Should they be thrown into the same grades as students whose educations were far advanced, or placed with younger white children whose level of learning was the same?

And there was "Where?" Assuming most school districts did not have the money to build a raft of new schools, would some white children then be forced to attend decrepit black schools?

None of these and many other questions had been addressed, let alone answered, and it would fall to Earl Warren and his fellow justices to try.

They would get no help from the attorneys. Thurgood Marshall and the other lawyers for the plaintiffs predictably asked that the decision be implemented immediately, that waiting would achieve nothing since the secessionist school districts would not implement plans for integration until they had to. The districts had said as much. The lawyers for the school districts asked for time, claiming they simply did not have the resources to change their entire way of educating children at the snap of a finger.

It took more than six weeks for Warren and his colleagues to come to a decision, and in many ways, it was not a decision at all. On May 31, 1955, the last day of the Court's term, Chief Justice Warren repeated that, since segregation was now unconstitutional, "All provisions of federal, state, or local law requiring or permitting such discrimination must yield to this principle." But he also acknowledged, "Full implementation of these constitutional principles may require solution of varied local school problems. School authorities have the primary responsibility for elucidating, assessing, and solving these problems; courts will have to consider whether the action of school authorities constitutes good faith implementation of the governing constitutional principles."

In other words, local school boards were responsible for coming up with plans, which local federal courts would decide were or were not "in good faith." "To that end," Warren wrote, "the courts may consider problems related to administration, arising from the physical condition of the school plant, the school transportation system, personnel, revision of school districts and attendance areas into compact units to achieve a system of determining admission to the public schools." If courts determined that local boards were trying to avoid compliance, what action would come next was not clear. Few federal judges were sufficiently experienced in education to come up with plans on their own, and delegating the task to local leaders promised to end in deadlock between white and black.

Warren also wrote in his opinion "that substantial steps to eliminate racial discrimination in public schools have already been taken, not only in some of the communities in which these cases arose, but . . . in other states as well." In this, the chief justice was painting an overly rosy picture. In fact, in Prince Edward County, whites would close down the school system entirely, set up private "academies" only for white children, and the public schools would stay closed for five years.

In the end, *Brown II*, as it came to be known, was best remembered for its vagueness, which was epitomized in the final paragraph:

> The cases are remanded to the District Courts to take such proceedings and enter such orders and decrees consistent with this opinion as are necessary and proper to admit to public schools on a racially nondiscriminatory basis with all deliberate speed the parties to these cases.

"All deliberate speed" became a phrase engraved in legal history. It often turned out to be no speed at all.

CHAPTER 23

Legacy

INTEGRATION PROVED AS difficult to implement as Herman Talmadge and other white supremacists predicted. In February 1956, Virginia senator Harry Byrd called for "massive resistance" in the South to challenge the Court's ruling. Although he claimed he was not advocating violence, he wanted "southern states to stand together in declaring the court's opinion unconstitutional." Byrd told his fellow whites, "If we can organize the southern states for massive resistance to this order I think that in time the rest of the country will realize that racial integration is not going to be accepted in the South." In Virginia, that included a law denying state funds for, and eventually closing, any school that chose to integrate.

The following month, more than one hundred Southern congressmen, all from states that had been a part of the

Confederacy, signed a "Declaration of Constitutional Principles," which became widely known as the Southern Manifesto. It attacked the Supreme Court for abusing its power and trampling on states' rights, and urged Southerners to use all "lawful means" to resist the "chaos and confusion" that would result from school desegregation.

No one in Congress spoke against it.

Although publicly urging Southerners to refrain from violence, Southern legislators knew that violence both in threat and reality would greet their pronouncements. While not every Southern community resisted integration, most did, at least at first. One such example is provided by research findings of the Equal Justice Initiative, founded in 1989 by famed black advocate Bryan Stevenson to provide "legal representation to people who have been illegally convicted, unfairly sentenced, or abused in state jails and prisons."

When the school board of Mansfield, Texas, a farming town of 1500 people, admitted 12 black students to all-white Mansfield High School, white residents took to the streets in protest. On August 30, 1956, the first day of school, mobs of white pro-segregationists patrolled the streets with guns and other weapons to prevent black children from registering.

The mob hung an African American effigy at the

top of the school's flagpole and set it on fire. Attached to each pant leg was a sign. One read, "This Negro tried to enter a white school. This would be a terrible way to die," and the other read, "Stay away, niggers." A second effigy was hung on the front of the school building. Soon afterward, the Mansfield School Board voted to "exhaust all legal remedies to delay integration." In December 1956, the United States Supreme Court ordered the Mansfield school district to integrate immediately, but Mansfield public schools did not officially desegregate until 1965.

Students of color who did succeed in attending integrated schools faced challenges of their own.

Whites pushed black students down stairs, shouted slurs at them in hallways, ostracized them in cafeterias, and left death threats in their lockers. When John F. Kennedy was murdered in 1963, white students in Baton Rouge formed a circle around the handful of blacks at their school and chanted, "We killed Lincoln, we killed Kennedy, and we'll kill anyone else who tries to help niggers."

Resistance to integration did not always come from whites. Many prominent African American educators, such

University of Alabama students burn desegregation literature, 1956.

as Georgia's Horace Tate, president of that state's black teachers association, had worked tirelessly to improve black education in segregated schools and were convinced that all-black schools were the best places to educate black students. Tate had begged and cajoled white officials for better facilities, engaged in fund-raising in both the North and the South, and helped recruit high-quality teachers who could provide the sort of personal attention to black students that they could never hope to get in white schools.

Tate was highly critical of the push to integration. "All change is not progress," he would say later. "We are facing a new kind of slavery." He would also claim "second-class integration" was "more evil than was segregation."

There was no question that the *Brown* decision had the same devastating impact on African American schools that the integration of Major League Baseball had on the Negro baseball leagues.

> Black schools were closed, leading to the dismissal of thousands of African-American teachers and principals; and black children were bussed to formerly all-white schools, which were sometimes inferior to the ones they had left . . . Even when black schools lacked textbooks and other essentials . . . dedicated educators like Tate

transformed them into truly educational institutions. At the schools he led, Tate knew every child by name. More than that, though, he knew how to "motivate the deprived child," to quote one of the speakers at Tate's teacher conventions. The white schools where black children were sent could not—or would not—do that.

Despite all the problems, integration took root across much of the South, and in the North as well, and was widely viewed as a positive force in improving the lives and futures of children of color. But integration had succeeded only as a result of the hundreds of lawsuits the LDF initiated to curb the delaying and avoidance tactics that whites attempted to employ.

After watching segregationists opt for one obvious ruse after another for the better part of a decade, the Supreme Court finally decided the time for "deliberate speed" had passed. The justices began to issue rulings that undercut segregationist schemes. In such cases as *Swann v. Charlotte-Mecklenburg*, in 1971, which affirmed the federal courts' constitutional authority to step in and order specific remedies to end state-sponsored segregation, and *Green v. County School Board*, in 1968, where the Court struck down a "freedom of choice" plan that kept schools segregated and insisted

*A classroom in Fort Myer Elementary School in Virginia
on the first day of desegregation, September 8, 1954.*

segregation be eradicated "root and branch," the justices
moved the nation closer to the ideals they had expressed in
Brown v. Board of Education.

But the Supreme Court's zeal in protecting integration

has waned over the years with a change in the roster of justices. In May 2019, UCLA's Civil Rights Project published a report, *Harming Our Common Future: America's Segregated Schools 65 Years after Brown*, which said:

> Intense levels of segregation—which had decreased markedly after 1954 for black students—are on the rise once again. In the 1990s, a series of Supreme Court decisions led to the end of hundreds of desegregation orders and plans across the nation. This report shows that the growth of racial and economic segregation that began then has now continued unchecked for nearly three decades, placing the promise of Brown at grave risk.

In one of those cases, *Parents Involved in Community Schools v. Seattle School District No. 1*, in 2007, Chief Justice John Roberts struck down a racial tiebreaker, one of a few used to determine which students would be accepted in schools outside their own geographic districts, writing:

> The way to stop discrimination on the basis of race is to stop discriminating on the basis of race.

Seven years later, Justice Sonia Sotomayor, in a dissent, countered:

> The way to stop discrimination on the basis of race
> is to speak openly and candidly on the subject of
> race, and to apply the Constitution with eyes open
> to the unfortunate effects of centuries of racial
> discrimination.

Many who saw the election of Barack Obama to the American presidency as signaling the end of the nation's racial divide have been stunned to realize it was perhaps worse when he left office than when he began. The nation has been forced to endure a stream of racially motivated terror attacks and murders that recall, for many, similar incidents during the Jim Crow era and the civil rights movement. Some have been controversial, involving the death of black men at the hands of white police officers, and others have been ghastly, as when a young white man calmly walked into a black church in South Carolina and gunned down nine people during a prayer service.

And so, the inevitable question: Was it all worth it?

The answer is a resounding yes.

Because for all the imperfections, for all the setbacks, for all the racism that is still sadly a far too prominent presence in American life, *Brown v. Board of Education* for the first time in the history of the United States stated without qualification that separating people, diminishing people, enslaving people simply because of the color of their skin was *wrong*. The Declaration of Independence hadn't done it; the Constitution hadn't done it; Congress hadn't done it; no president had done it; and the Supreme Court hadn't done it. In the decades after *Brown*, America may not have made the progress most would have wanted, but without the *Brown* decision, no progress of any kind would have been possible.

BIBLIOGRAPHY

Online Resources

https://www.aft.org/periodical/american-educator/summer-2004/jim-crows-schools.

https://web.archive.org/web/20090122230015/http://naacp.org/about/history/howbegan/index.htm.

https://www.archives.gov/exhibits/documented-rights/exhibit/section5/detail/briggs-dissent-transcript.html.

https://www.baltimoremagazine.com/2017/8/7/justice-for-all-50-years-after-thurgood-marshall-supreme-court-confirmation.

https://www.blackpast.org/african-american-history/national-association-advancement-colored-people-and-long-struggle-civil-rights-united-s/.

https://www.civilrightsproject.ucla.edu/research/k-12-education/integration-and-diversity/harming-our-common-future-americas-segregated-schools-65-years-after-brown/Brown-65-050919v4-final.pdf.

http://credo.library.umass.edu/view/full/mums312-b157-i205. (Niagara Movement)

https://digital.library.vcu.edu/digital/collection/voices/id/10. (Content removed from website.)

https://eji.org/history-racial-injustice-resistance-to-school-desegregation.

https://www.eiu.edu/past_tracker/AfricanAmerican_Independent65_3Sept1908_RaceWarInTheNorth.pdf. (Springfield riot of 1908)

https://harvardmagazine.com/2018/07/moorfield-storey.

https://www.history.com/news/761st-tank-battalion-black-panthers-liberators-battle-of-the-bulge.

https://historyengine.richmond.edu/episodes/view/4682.

https://www.historynet.com.

https://www.kansascity.com/news/local/article107490072.html. (Esther Brown)

https://www.law.cornell.edu/houston/housbio.htm.

https://www.loc.gov/exhibits/brown/index.html.

https://www.loc.gov/exhibits/civil-rights-act/index.html.

https://www.loc.gov/exhibits/naacp/index.html.

https://www.modjourn.org/journal/crisis.

http://nationalhumanitiescenter.org/pds/maai3/segregation/text2/investigatelynchings.pdf.

https://www.nybooks.com/articles/2018/11/22/brown-segregation-without-deliberate-speed/.

http://www.scencyclopedia.org/sce/entries/waring-julius-waties/.

https://www.sj-r.com/news/20180814/1908-springfield-race-riot-led-to-creation-of-naacp.

https://www.smithsonianmag.com/history/death-hundreds-elaine-massacre-led-supreme-court-take-major-step-toward-equal-justice-african-americans-180969863/.

http://theconversation.com/black-troops-were-welcome-in-britain-but-jim-crow-wasnt-the-race-riot-of-one-night-in-june-1943-98120.

https://thetandd.com/news/opinion/pink-franklin-naacp-s-first-legal-case/article_accf63f0-de0c-11e3-acf6-0019bb2963f4.html.

https://www.thirteen.org/wnet/jimcrow/stories_events_moore.html.

https://www.trumanlibrary.gov/.

https://tshaonline.org/handbook/online/articles/fsw23.

http://www2.vcdh.virginia.edu/saxon/servlet/SaxonServlet?source=/
xml_docs/modernva/modernva_transcripts.xml&style=/xml_docs/
modernva/interview_modernva.xsl&level=single&id=Oliver_Hill.
(Barbara Johns and the student strike)

https://www.vqronline.org/essay/unacknowledged-lesson-earl-warren-
and-japanese-relocation-controversy.

Books and Articles

"Oral History: A Symposium on Charles Hamilton Houston." *New England Law Review*, Vol. 27 (Spring 1993).

Arsenault, Raymond. *Freedom Riders: 1961 and the Struggle for Racial Justice*. New York: Oxford University Press, 2006.

Bahr, Diana M. *The Unquiet Nisei: An Oral History of the Life of Sue Kunitomi Embrey*. New York: Palgrave, 2007.

Billington, Monroe. "Civil Rights, President Truman and the South." *Journal of Negro History*, Vol. 58, No. 2 (April 1973).

Burke, W. Lewis. "*Pink Franklin v. South Carolina*: The NAACP's First Case." *American Journal of Legal History*, Vol. 54, No. 3 (July 2014).

Casas, Martha. "An Historical Analysis of the United States Supreme Court and Its Adjudication of *Gong Lum v. Rice* (1927) and *Keyes v. Denver School District No. 1* (1973)." *Journal of Thought*, Vol. 41, No. 4 (Winter 2006).

Cho, Sumi K. "Redeeming Whiteness in the Shadow of Internment: Earl Warren, *Brown*, and a Theory of Racial Redemption." *Boston College Third World Law Journal*, Vol. 19, No. 1 (1998).

Cray, Ed. *Chief Justice: A Biography of Earl Warren*. New York: Simon & Schuster, 1997.

Crouthamel, James L. "The Springfield Race Riot of 1908." *Journal of Negro History*, Vol. 45, No. 3 (July 1960).

Du Bois, W. E. Burghardt. *The Amenia Conference: An Historical Negro Gathering*. Amenia, NY: Troutbeck Press, 1925.

———. *Souls of Black Folk: Essays and Sketches*. Chicago: A. C. McClurg, 1903.

Dudziak, Mary L. "The Limits of Good Faith: Desegregation in Topeka, Kansas, 1950–1956." *Law and History Review*, Vol. 5 (1987).

Elliott, Mark. "Race, Color Blindness, and the Democratic Public: Albion W. Tourgée's Radical Principles in *Plessy v. Ferguson*." *Journal of Southern History*, Vol. 67, No. 2 (May 2001).

Forth, Christopher E. "Booker T. Washington and the 1905 Niagara Movement Conference." *Journal of Negro History*, Vol. 72, No. 3/4 (Summer-Autumn, 1987).

Goldstone, Dwonna. "'I Don't Believe in Segregation': *Sweatt v. Painter* and the Groundwork for *Brown v. Board of Education*." *Judges' Journal*, Vol. 43, No. 2 (2004).

Henkin, Louis. "*Shelley v. Kraemer*: Notes for a Revised Opinion." *University of Pennsylvania Law Review*, Vol. 110, No. 4 (February 1962).

Henry, Patrick. "Jackie Robinson: Athlete and American Par Excellence." *Virginia Quarterly Review*, Vol. 73, No. 2 (Spring 1997).

Hine, Darlene Clark. "The *Briggs v. Elliott* Legacy: Black Culture, Consciousness, and Community before *Brown*, 1930–1954." *University of Illinois Law Review* 2004, No. 5.

Houston, Charles H. "The Need for Negro Lawyers." *Journal of Negro Education*, Vol. 4, No. 1 (January 1935).

Jones, Douglas L. "The Sweatt Case and the Development of Legal Education for Negroes in Texas." *Texas Law Review*, Vol. 47 (March 1969).

Katznelson, Ira. *Fear Itself: The New Deal and the Origins of Our Time*. New York: Liveright Publishing, 2013.

Kent, Charles A. *Memoir of Henry Billings Brown, Late Justice of the*

Supreme Court of the United States, Consisting of an Autobiographical Sketch. New York: Vail-Ballou Company, 1915.

Kluger, Richard. *Simple Justice: The History of* Brown v. Board of Education *and Black America's Struggle for Equality*. New York: Vintage Books, 2004.

Kolb, Wade III. "*Briggs v. Elliott* Revisited: A Study in Grassroots Activism and Trial Advocacy from the Early Civil Rights Era." *Journal of Southern Legal History*, Vol. 19 (January 2011).

Locke, Alain, ed. *The New Negro: An Interpretation*. New York: Albert and Charles Boni, 1925.

Mack, Kenneth. *Representing the Race: The Creation of the Civil Rights Lawyer*. Cambridge, MA: Harvard University Press, 2012.

McNeil, Genna Rae. "Charles Hamilton Houston." *Black Law Journal*, Vol. 3 (Spring 1974).

Moskos, Charles C., Jr. "The American Dilemma in Uniform: Race in the Armed Forces." *Annals of the American Academy of Political and Social Science*, Vol. 406 (March 1973).

Pethia, Theodore J., and George J. Thomas. "The Beginning of the End of the Separate but Equal Doctrine." *Catholic University Law Review*, Vol. 1, No. 2 (1951).

Robinson, Jackie, with Alfred Duckett. *I Never Had It Made: An Autobiography of Jackie Robinson*. New York: HarperCollins, 2013.

Rudwick, Elliott M. "The National Negro Committee Conference of 1909." *Phylon Quarterly*, Vol. 18, No. 4 (4th Quarter 1957).

———. "The Niagara Movement." *Journal of Negro History*, Vol. 42, No. 3 (July 1957).

Smith, Ronald A. "The Paul Robeson–Jackie Robinson Saga and a Political Collision." *Journal of Sport History*, Vol. 6, No. 2 (Summer 1979).

Tushnet, Mark. "Lawyer Thurgood Marshall." *Stanford Law Review*, Vol. 44 (Summer 1992).

Tygiel, Jules. *Baseball's Great Experiment: Jackie Robinson and His Legacy.* New York: Oxford University Press, 1997.

White, Walter. *A Man Called White: The Autobiography of Walter White.* New York: 1948 Viking, 1948.

Wells-Barnett, Ida B. *Lynch Law in Georgia: A Six-Weeks' Record in the Center of Southern Civilization, as Faithfully Chronicled by the "Atlanta Journal" and the "Atlanta Constitution."* Chicago: Chicago Colored Citizens, 1899.

Whitman, Leanna Lee, and Michael Hayes. "Lou Pollak: The Road to *Brown v. Board of Education* and Beyond." *Proceedings of the American Philosophical Society*, Vol. 158, No. 1 (March 2014).

Wilson, Paul E. "Ad Astra per Aspera: *Brown v. Board of Education of Topeka." University of Missouri at Kansas City Law Review*, Vol. 68 (2000).

———. "The Genesis of *Brown v. Board of Education." Kansas Journal of Law & Public Policy*, Vol. 7 (1996).

Wilson, Woodrow. *A History of the American People*, Documentary Edition, Vol. 9, 1902, p. 58.

SOURCE NOTES

Chapter 1: Separate

"Substantial equality of rights . . ." Hall v. DeCuir, 95 U.S. 503 (1877).

"The [Separate Car Law] itself is a skillful attempt to confuse . . ." Quoted in Mark Elliott, "Race, Color Blindness, and the Democratic Public: Albion W. Tourgée's Radical Principles in *Plessy v. Ferguson,*" *Journal of Southern History*, Vol. 67, No. 2 (May 2001), p. 291.

"The gist of our case . . . equal accommodation." Ibid., p. 306.

"I was of a New England Puritan family . . ." Charles A. Kent, *Memoir of Henry Billings Brown, Late Justice of the Supreme Court of the United States, Consisting of an Autobiographical Sketch* (New York: Vail-Ballou Company, 1915), p. 1.

"The rooms, though not particularly uncomfortable . . . Sunday was compulsory." Ibid., pp. 11–12.

"The Thirteenth Amendment . . . of the two races." 163 U.S. 542-3 (1896).

"In the nature of things . . ." Ibid.

"The argument also assumes that social prejudices . . ." 163 U.S. 551-2 (1896).

"It is said in argument . . ." Ibid.

"In view of the Constitution, in the eye of the law . . ." Ibid.

Chapter 2: Land of Lincoln

Between 1890 and 1903, 1,889 lynchings . . . to 80 percent. Lynching records were compiled by the Tuskegee Institute beginning in 1882 through a study of articles and other records. The material is currently in the university's archives.

"During six weeks of the months of March . . ." Ida B. Wells-Barnett, *Lynch Law in Georgia: A Six-Weeks' Record in the Center of Southern Civilization, as Faithfully Chronicled by the "Atlanta Journal" and the "Atlanta Constitution"* (Chicago: Chicago Colored Citizens, 1899), p. 2.

"The capital had a reputation, partly justified . . ." James Crouthamel, "The Springfield Race Riot of 1908," *Journal of Negro History*, Vol. 45, No. 3 (July 1960), p. 164.

"cut to pieces by a wild negro . . . in this city." *Neshoba (MS) Democrat*, July 9, 1908, p. 2.

"was awakened by the presence . . . arrival of the police." Ibid.

"Lodge Members Strung Up . . . Negro tenant, Rufus Browder." *Clarksburg (WV) Telegram*, August 6, 1908, p. 5.

"dragged from her bed . . . a lynching bee." *Palestine (TX) Daily Herald*, August 14, 1908, p. 1.

"scores of worthless and lawless Negroes." Crouthamel, "Springfield," p. 168.

"Curse the day . . ." Crouthamel, p. 170.

"a plump, middle-aged widow . . ." Ibid., p. 170.

"Organized groups methodically decimated . . ." https://www.sj-r.com/news/20180814/1908-springfield-race-riot-led-to-creation-of-naacp.

"Any Negro unlucky enough . . ." Crouthamel, "Springfield," p. 173.

"By breakfast time, about 1,800 militia . . ." Ibid., p. 174.

"Many firms discharged their Negro help . . ." Ibid.

Chapter 3: Resistance

"The white men of the South . . ." Woodrow Wilson, *A History of the American People*, Documentary Edition, Vol. 9, 1902, p. 58.

"No suffrage, no nigger." Kent, *Memoir*, p. 113.

"This is indeed a happy day . . ." Ibid.

"I here declare the so-called 'race question' . . ." *New York Times*, September 19, 1895, p. 1.

"The selection of Booker T. Washington . . ." *Indianapolis Sunday Journal*, September 15, 1895, part 2, p. 12.

"In all things that are purely social . . ." Ibid., p.5.

"The wisest among my race . . ." Ibid.

"When [men] think of American freedom . . ." *New York Times*, September 19, 1895, p. 4.

"His efforts at appeasement . . ." Louis R. Harlan, "The Secret Life of Booker T. Washington," *Journal of Southern History*, Vol. 37, No. 3 (August 1971), p. 396.

"Of Mr. Booker T. Washington and Others . . . theories have gained." W. E. B. Du Bois, *Souls of Black Folk: Essays and Sketches* (Chicago: A. C. McClurg, 1903), pp. 42, 45, 58–59.

"His doctrine has tended to make . . ." Ibid.

"The Niagara Movement was the first national . . ." Elliott M. Rudwick, "The Niagara Movement," *Journal of Negro History*, Vol. 42, No. 3 (July 1957), p. 177.

"Since the day of its inception . . ." Ibid., p. 181–82.

He used all his influence . . . what Du Bois was doing. Ibid.

"We claim for ourselves . . ." https://teachingamericanhistory.org/library/document/niagara-movement-speech/.

Chapter 4: From the Ashes in Springfield

"Illinois Mobs Kill and Burn . . . Sixth Victim Dies." *New York Times*, August 15–17, 1908, all p. 1.

"Including many women and children . . ." https://www.eiu.edu/past_tracker/AfricanAmerican_Independent65_3Sept1908_RaceWarInTheNorth.pdf.

"For four years I had been studying . . ." https://web.archive.org/web/20090122230015/http://naacp.org/about/history/howbegan/index.htm.

Villard extended an invitation . . . W. E. B. Du Bois. http://credo.library.

umass.edu/view/pageturn/mums312-b287-i004/#page/3/mode/1up; also in Elliott M. Rudwick, "The National Negro Committee Conference of 1909," *Phylon Quarterly*, Vol. 18, No. 4 (4th Quarter, 1957), p. 414.

The conference drew three hundred . . . *New York Times*, June 1, 1909, p. 2.

"Mary White Ovington suggested to Walling . . . on the Advisory Committee." http://credo.library.umass.edu/view/full/mums312-b157-i205. (Niagara Movement)

"We denounce the ever-growing oppression . . . education for the most gifted." https://www.loc.gov/exhibits/naacp/founding-and-early-years.html.

For president, the group chose Moorfield Storey . . . including Native Americans. https://harvardmagazine.com/2018/07/moorfield-storey.

"When W. E. B. Du Bois founded *The Crisis* . . ." http://www.modjourn. org/render.php?view=mjp_object&id=crisiscollection.

"The object of this publication is . . ." https://library.brown.edu/ pdfs/127470517978125.pdf.

"What is the National Association for the . . ." https://library.brown.edu/ pdfs/1274705515484375.pdf.

Chapter 5: To the Courts

Although that crusade would eventually lead . . . Details of the Pink Franklin case can be found at https://thetandd.com/news/opinion/ pink-franklin-naacp-s-first-legal-case/article_accf63f0-de0c-11e3-acf6-0019bb2963f4.html; also in W. Lewis Burke, *"Pink Franklin v. South Carolina*: The NAACP's First Case," *American Journal of Legal History*, Vol. 54, No. 3 (July 2014), pp. 265–301; and in *The Crisis*, at https:// library.brown.edu/pdfs/1274705515484375.pdf.

"If the law is based on common sense . . . justice be done." *The Crisis*, https://modjourn.org/journal/crisis.

A number of state voting officials, all Democrats . . . *Daily Ardmoreite* (OK), February 5, 1911, p. 9.

When the case came to trial, another Republican . . . was unconstitutional. Franklin's paper the statesman, (Denver), June 17, 1911, p. 3.

"repugnant to the Fifteenth Amendment . . ." 238 U.S. 347 (1915).

"The death of Mr. Washington marks . . ." W. E. B. Du Bois, *The Amenia Conference: An Historical Negro Gathering* (Amenia, NY: Troutbeck Press, 1925), p. 4.

"the common law right of every landowner . . ." 245 U.S. 60 (1917).

Chapter 6: The Red Summer

"By the God of Heaven . . ." *The Crisis* (May 1919), Vol. 18, No. 1, p. 14.

"I was frequently whipped and also . . ." https://www.thirteen.org/wnet/ jimcrow/stories_events_moore.html. (*Moore v. Dempsey*)

"one of the most brilliant newspapermen . . ." Walter White, *A Man Called White: The Autobiography of Walter White.* 1948 Viking, p. 50.

"If the whole case is a mask . . ." 261 U.S. 86 (1923).

"I walked down West Cherry Street . . . pass for white no more." http://nationalhumanitiescenter.org/pds/maai3/segregation/text2/ investigatelynchings.pdf.

Chapter 7: Passing the Torch: The New Negro Movement

"For generations in the mind of America . . . a spiritual emancipation." Alain Locke, ed., *The New Negro: An Interpretation* (New York: Albert and Charles Boni, 1925), p. 3.

"As a Second Lieutenant overseas, he encountered . . ." Genna Rae McNeil, "Charles Hamilton Houston," *Black Law Journal*, Vol. 3 (Spring 1974), p. 123.

"The hate and scorn showered on us . . ." https://www.law.cornell.edu/ houston/housbio.htm.

"The social justification for the Negro lawyer . . . 90,000 Negroes." Charles H. Houston, "The Need for Negro Lawyers," *Journal of Negro Education*, Vol. 4, No. 1 (January 1935), p. 49.

When Johnson accepted the job . . . called "Dummies Retreat." Richard Kluger, *Simple Justice: The History of* Brown v. Board of Education *and Black America's Struggle for Equality* (New York: Vintage Books, 2004), p. 123.

"I can tell most of the time . . ." Ibid., p. 125.

"Despite criticism, he insisted on . . ." The comments are Houston's, quoted in McNeil, "Charles Hamilton Houston," p. 124.

"a transformation which ordinarily . . ." Ibid.

Chapter 8: The Challenge

"The case reduces itself . . ." 275 U.S. 78 (1927).

"The homes of rural Negro youth are . . ." https://www.aft.org/periodical/american-educator/summer-2004/jim-crows-schools.

"A typical rural Negro school is . . . an rat, an boot." Ibid.

Chapter 9: To the Courts Once More

"Doctors can bury their . . . about being Negroes." Kluger, *Simple Justice*, p. 127.

"boldly challenge the constitutional . . ." https://www.loc.gov/exhibits/naacp/the-great-depression.html.

"His report stayed with me . . ." Kluger, *Simple Justice*, p. 136.

Chapter 10: Thurgood Marshall Joins the Fray

"I can still see him coming . . ." Kluger, *Simple Justice*, p. 173.

"Marshall later said his father . . ." https://www.baltimoremagazine.com/2017/8/7/justice-for-all-50-years-after-thurgood-marshall-supreme-court-confirmation.

"Marshall was a rare combination . . ." Ibid.

Chapter 11: Setbacks

"president of his senior class, an honors graduate . . ." . . . Missouri Law School. *New York Times*, July 11, 2009, p. 19.

White, racist Democrats, especially in the Senate . . . labor was concentrated.) To read about the New Deal and racist Southerners, see Ira Katznelson's excellent *Fear Itself: The New Deal and the Origins of Our Time* (New York: Liveright Publishing, 2013).

Chapter 12: No Turning Back

In one English town, when US . . . http://theconversation.com/
black-troops-were-welcome-in-britain-but-jim-crow-wasnt-the-race-riot-
of-one-night-in-june-1943-98120.

"I knew then that I wasn't . . ." https://www.thirteen.org/wnet/jimcrow/
stories_events_ww2.html.

"tells the story of 140,000 Black . . . None of us were." http://
theconversation.com/black-troops-were-welcome-in-britain-but-jim-
crow-wasnt-the-race-riot-of-one-night-in-june-1943-98120.

"something drastic has got . . ." https://www.loc.gov/exhibits/naacp/
world-war-ii-and-the-post-war-years.html.

"We, as colored Americans are . . ." https://historyengine.richmond.edu/
episodes/view/4682.

"I was aware of the fact that . . ." Jackie Robinson with Alfred Duckett,
I Never Had It Made: An Autobiography of Jackie Robinson (New York:
HarperCollins, 2013), p. 19.

"A man of principle. . . ." https://www.nydailynews.com/news/
jackie-words-echo-years-article-1.210438.

Chapter 13: Renewing the Attack

"He touched me . . ." Raymond Arsenault, *Freedom Riders: 1961 and the
Struggle for Racial Justice* (New York: Oxford University Press, 2006), p. 13.

"It seems clear to us . . ." 328 U.S. 373 (1946).

The Court acknowledged that . . . by state courts. 334 U.S. 1 (1948).

Chapter 14: A School of One's Own

To become a supervisor, a postal worker . . . a lawyer himself. https://
tshaonline.org/handbook/online/articles/fsw23.

In 1940, there were 7,570 white lawyers . . . Douglas L. Jones, "The
Sweatt Case and the Development of Legal Education for Negroes in
Texas," *Texas Law Review*, Vol. 47 (March 1969), p. 677.

"secured the law offices and . . ." Ibid., p. 682.

"had a Constitutional duty to provide . . ." 339 U.S. 637 (1950).

"The legal education offered . . ." 339 U.S. 629 (1950).

"The restrictions imposed upon appellant . . ." 339 U.S. 637 (1950).

"If the two cases are considered together . . ." Theodore J. Pethia and George J. Thomas, "The Beginning of the End of the 'Separate but Equal' Doctrine," *Catholic University Law Review*, Vol. 1, No. 2 (1951), p. 73.

Chapter 15: The Main Event

"We ain't got no money . . ." Wade Kolb III, "*Briggs v. Elliott* Revisited: A Study in Grassroots Activism and Trial Advocacy from the Early Civil Rights Era," *Journal of Southern Legal History*, Vol.19 (January 2011), p. 123.

"Shall we suffer endless persecution . . ." Darlene Clark Hine, "The *Briggs v. Elliott* Legacy: Black Culture, Consciousness, and Community before Brown, 1930–1954," *University of Illinois Law Review, No. 5* (2004), p. 1063.

"In 1944, he began handing down . . ." http://www.scencyclopedia.org/sce/entries/waring-julius-waties/.

"I am of the opinion that . . ." https://www.archives.gov/exhibits/documented-rights/exhibit/section5/detail/briggs-dissent-transcript.html.

"In '55 my father was given . . ." https://www.nytimes.com/2004/01/18/education/the-cases-when-schools-were-shacks.html?searchResultPosition=5.

Chapter 16: Student Revolt

"There was no running water . . . crawling around." NYT, January 18, 2004, Section A. p. 4.

"I came to realize . . ." https://digital.library.vcu.edu/digital/collection/voices/id/10. [Content removed from website.]

"It seemed like reaching for . . ." Kluger, *Simple Justice*, p. 477.

Chapter 17: Kansas

Only one hotel in the city . . . swim there as well. Kluger, *Simple Justice*, pp. 375–76.

"following World War II, a new generation . . ." Paul E. Wilson, "The Genesis of *Brown v. Board of Education*," *Kansas Journal of Law & Public Policy*, Vol. 7 (1996), p. 10.

"In order for Linda to catch . . ." Ibid., p. 18.

"All of a sudden we seem . . ." https://www.kansascity.com/news/local/article107490072.html. (Ester Brown)

"I'm just a Kansas housewife . . . a fair shake." Ibid.

"Segregation of white and colored children . . ." Trial transcript at 245–46, *Brown v. Board of Educ.*, 98 F. Supp. 797 (D. Kan.1951).

Chapter 18: The Battle Is Joined

"The Supreme Court chamber . . ." *New York Times*, December 10, 1952, p. 1.

"the court should not set aside . . ." *New York Times*, December 11, 1952, p. 1.

"We submit that in this case . . ." Kluger, *Simple Justice*, p. 583.

"people who were imported . . . to respect." 60 U.S. 393 (1857).

Chapter 19: A Change at the Top

"If anyone ever clinched . . ." Ed Cray, *Chief Justice: A Biography of Earl Warren* (New York: Simon & Schuster, 1887), p. 240.

"the Declaration of Independence and . . ." https://www.sfchronicle.com/news/article/Calif-officials-including-Earl-Warren-once-13437345.php.

"executed this mission . . . could be easily compared." Sumi K. Cho, "Redeeming Whiteness in the Shadow of Internment: Earl Warren, *Brown*, and a Theory of Racial Redemption," *Boston College Third World Law Journal*, Vol. 19, No. 1 (1998), p. 93.

"The Japanese situation as it . . ." Ibid., p. 92.

"distribution of the Japanese . . . inclined to do so." Ibid.

"deeply regretted the removal order . . ." Diana M. Bahr, *The Unquiet Nisei: An Oral History of the Life of Sue Kunitomi Embrey* (New York: Palgrave, 2007), p. 143.

Chapter 21: The Meaning of Equality

"These cases come to us . . . consolidated opinion." 347 U.S. 483 (1954).

"Re-argument was largely devoted . . . with which we are faced." Ibid.

"In approaching this problem . . . equal protection of the laws." Ibid.

"Education is perhaps the most important . . . on equal terms." Ibid.

"We come then to the question . . . that it does." Ibid.

"To separate them from others . . . to be undone." Ibid.

New York Times columnist James Reston . . . *New York Times*, May 18, 1954, p. 14.

"We conclude that . . . Fourteenth Amendment." 347 U.S. 483 (1954).

Chapter 22: Making It Real

"there will never be mixed schools . . . bloodshed" *New York Times*, May 18, 1954, p. 1.

"We will use the courts . . ." Ibid., p. 16.

"Neither the atom bomb nor . . ." *Chicago Defender* quoted in Ibid., p. 19.

"All provisions of federal, state, or local . . ." 349 U.S. 294 (1955).

Chapter 23: Legacy

"If we can organize the southern states . . ." *New York Times*, February 26, 1956, p. 1.

"When the school board of Mansfield . . . desegregate until 1965." https://eji.org/history-racial-injustice-resistance-to-school-desegregation.

"Whites pushed black students down . . ." https://www.nybooks.com/articles/2018/11/22/brown-segregation-without-deliberate-speed/.

"All change is not progress . . . than was segregation." https://eji.org/
history-racial-injustice-resistance-to-school-desegregation.

"Black schools were closed . . .—or would not—do that." https://www
.nybooks.com/articles/2018/11/22/brown-segregation-without-deliberate-
speed/.

"In such cases as *Swann v. Charlotte-Mecklenburg . . . Brown v. Board
of Education.*" 391 U.S. 430 (1968).

"Intense levels of segregation . . ." https://www.civilrightsproject.ucla.
edu/research/k-12-education/integration-and-diversity/harming-our-
common-future-americas-segregated-schools-65-years-after-brown/
Brown-65-050919v4-final.pdf.

"The way to stop discrimination . . . basis of race." 555 U.S. 701 (2007).

"The way to stop discrimination . . . racial discrimination." 572 U.S. 291
(2014).

PHOTOGRAPH AND ILLUSTRATION CREDITS

INDEX

Note: Page numbers in *italics* refer to illustrations.

ACKNOWLEDGMENTS

Once again, I want to express my deepest appreciation to Scholastic—to David Levithan, Lizette Serrano, the amazing Emily Heddleson, Amy Goppert, Danielle Yadao, Ellie Berger, and Dick Robinson—for their commitment, support, and enthusiasm in publishing stories that need to be told for an audience that very much needs to hear them. And thanks to Amy Chan and Jael Fogle, who helped bring this book to fruition. As for my editor, Lisa Sandell—it is common these days in publishing to say, "They just don't make them like that anymore." Well, they do. My agent, Charlie Olsen, is always there when I need him and laughs at my jokes, each of which can be a thankless chore.

And, of course, my wife, Nancy, my daughter, Lee, and, by the time this is published, my son-in-law, Tyler, all of whom pretend I'm easy to get along with.

ABOUT THE AUTHOR

LAWRENCE GOLDSTONE is the author of *Stolen Justice: The Struggle for African American Voting Rights*, of which *School Library Journal* wrote in a starred review: "Goldstone has provided new and compelling insight into the societal impact of the U.S. Supreme Court's decisions related to voting rights. A must-buy for all high school collections," and *Unpunished Murder: Massacre at Colfax and the Quest for Justice*, which a *Booklist* starred review called "gripping . . . and a well-informed perspective on American history. Spotlighting an event seldom discussed in books for young people, Goldstone provides a complex, useful historical context for understanding issues surrounding race and justice." He is also the author of more than a dozen books for adults, including four on constitutional law.

He lives in Sagaponack, New York, with his wife, medieval and Renaissance historian Nancy Goldstone.